NOT

HOW TO FAIL IN BUSINESS

WITHOUT EVEN TRYING

Bob Boze
and
Robyn Bennett

Advanced Reviews

What business owners are saying about *How Not to Fail in Business Without Really Trying*

"I enjoyed reading this book – each section followed each other quite nicely. I also enjoyed the "exercises" bit at the end of each section. This helped me to put the reading into practise and made me understand what one needs to do for going into business."

Anita Lewis, Business owner wanna be, New Zealand

"This is an EXCELLENT read (even ESSENTIAL) for anyone thinking about being their own boss! Laugh out loud in places, followed by very sobering insights encouraging follow up by the reader to develop a pragmatic, dependable and valuable business plan and move from using 'rose tinted dream glasses' to the clear sight of reality. Wish I had had it 15 years ago!! Well done Robyn and Bob!"

Tricia Caughley, AAPNZ Fellow, Ex business owner and Senior Administrator, Retired, Wellington, New Zealand

"This is an easy-to-read book (thank you), humorous (also thank you), and rich with helpful examples (I'll be dreaming of cupcakes tonight for sure!). Being a business owner myself, many things resonated with me. In fact, I had a few 'Crap! I never thought of that!' moments. The big lesson here for me was 'Start small and expand!' Looking back on the lifespan of my business, I wish I had done that. Instead, I went big immediately with nowhere to go from there. So happy I stumbled upon this wonderful book! It will come in handy for my next business venture."

Carly Fanguy, Co-Owner, 57 Degrees, San Diego, Ca.

"An amazingly written book, that highlights key points of starting a business, including the hard stuff. Bob and Robyn make you feel at ease with sarcasm and jokes; to really take you out of the stress and help you think with a level head."

Alicia Melbourne, Owner of Maria Veni and (coming soon) Enchanted Cocktails, Alnwick, England

First edition published 2018

ISBN-13: 9781723716775 (Softcover)

About The Authors

Combined, the authors have over 50 years of experience in both industry and small business.

Bob Boze started his career in aerospace as a project engineer, progressed to project management and then into senior management. After 15 years, he left industry to open a home repair and renovation company and two years later became a partner in a restaurant.

Five years after that he returned to senior management, working in the airline industry while still running his renovation company on a part time basis and eventually retiring after seven years with Home Depot in plumbing sales.

Over his various careers he has gained extensive experience in training, as well as technical and commercial customer service with the airlines, retail home repair and the hospitality industries.

Retiring in 2012, he fulfilled his dream to become a writer and now has four published books; a romance trilogy and his autobiography.

After living in two foreign countries and three states, Bob now resides in Bonita, in the beautiful south bay area of San Diego, California.

***

Robyn Bennett started her career in administration working mainly as an executive assistant to senior management. In 2000 she used her vast knowledge and experience to establish a secretarial business providing executive secretarial services to organizations and individuals. At the same time she was being sourced for her skills and set up an additional business, Team Link Training, providing training in office administration.

In 2005 she wound up the secretarial business to focus solely on training. By 2017 she had run over 1,000 courses in both the public and private sectors, the most popular being minute taking. In addition, she became a popular presenter at conferences both in New Zealand and Australia.

From 2003-2013 she ran the often sold-out Northern Administrators' Summit, which was a two-day conference aimed at PAs/EAs (Personal and Executive Assistants) and administrators.

Like Bob, Robyn is also a published author. In 2017 she published *Minute Taking Madness*, a resource book for minute takers, as well as two romance novels.

In addition to *How Not to Fail in Business Without Even Trying*, they are also working on a co-author romance novel, Robyn's autobiography, which describes her rise through the working world to become a PA and eventually open her own businesses. They are also helping each other with three more romance novels.

Robyn lives in the beautiful picturesque town of Blenheim, New Zealand.

Forward

This book is intended to help you in planning, starting and successfully running your own business. It is by no means a complete guide to everything you need to do in order to be successful. Only you can determine exactly what you need to do in planning, establishing and operating your specific business.

What we've tried to do is help you to conceptualize your ideas into an outline, expand that concept from an outline into a rough business plan and from there address areas common to most businesses.

Finally, we've tried to give as many examples as possible, using a variety of business types, to help you think about how each section may apply to your specific business. To that end, we have included various stories from our own personal experience and that of friends, so you will know you're not alone and perhaps learn from our experiences.

A few warnings. First, we'll do our best to help guide you but, you have to do the work! If you're looking for a cookie cutter plan, this isn't it. If you want someone to tell you how to run your business, go look in the mirror. If you want to know who will make your business successful, go look in the mirror. If you don't think that's the right person, you need to seriously reconsider opening your own business!

No book can make your business run smoothly or be successful. Only you can do that! All we can do is get the gears moving and stir up ideas. It's up to you to choose which ones might work for you and which ones you couldn't care less about.

Our second warning is about us as writers. We've often been described as weird and our sense of humor as even weirder. We also firmly believe that, as a business owner, your sense of humor will become your most valuable survival tool. So if you make it past this "Forward", you'll find we have tried to make our book as "unserious" as we can. This, we hope, does three things; makes you love us as writers, laugh a lot, and finally, reduce some of the stress in planning your business.

If we didn't give you a free copy, thank you for buying our book and let's get on with planning your business!

One last thing. The opinions expressed in this book are mostly ours (Duh? Who else's would they be?) Actually, in some rare cases others may've convinced us that their opinions were better than ours so, we may have adopted their opinion as our own. Since we can't remember whose opinion was whose, we have claimed them all as ours and take full responsibility and credit for all the wonderful stuff in this book. If you disagree with anything we've said, please feel free to email us and tell us why we're wrong. We're always open to new opinions and ideas.

Contents

Introduction

So why are we writing this book? What in the world possessed us to jump in the middle of your dream of opening your own business and give you advice? Better yet, who the hell are we and what makes us qualified to give you advice?

All excellent questions. If you're already asking yourself these and other questions you're off to a great start. If you're not, you really might want to think twice about owning a business and stick to working for someone else. Why? Because the first thing you'll learn about starting a business is to ask lots and lots of questions. If you think you already know most of what you need to open your business we'll bet half of what you're investing that you'll not make it through the first year.

However, since you're reading our book you either think we're great writers (in which case we love you, but you're beyond our help) or you already have a ton of questions and are off to a great start (in which case we think we can help).

What in the world ever possessed us to write this? You have to promise not to laugh! Aside from both of us being avid readers of romance and almost anything else, Bob was also hooked on watching Restaurant Impossible, Restaurant Stakeout, Bar Rescue, Hotel Rescue and several other business "rescue" shows. Oh, and he likes cheesy vampire books too. Robyn liked to keep her eye on local businesses and could accurately pick the lifespan of them based on two critical success factors, which are highlighted in Chapter 1.

Why? We really have no idea why Robyn developed her business crystal ball or what attracted Bob to watching those shows, but what interested both of them was their amazement at how little the people knew about their businesses! How can you own a restaurant and have no idea what food costs are? How can you own a bar and think that drinking with your customers is the only skill set you need? How can you own a hotel where the maid forgets to set out clean towels and no one notices? How can you own a business and not pay attention to the factors critical to your success?

Ah, but everyone knows the shows are just drama and problems created so people will watch the show, you say. Wrong! Which brings us to why we decided to inject ourselves (with your permission) into your dream and why Bob convinced Robyn to help him write this book. Simply put we want to help keep you from letting your business grow into a nightmare and you becoming the next star of Restaurant or Business Impossible or another statistic in failed small businesses.

Trust us, the people on those shows exist. They are just like you and us. People with a dream that's been growing in the back of their head: born out of frustration, a business they inherited, a skill they possess, an idea of how to do something better, a desire to make a fortune, a link to something they see missing, a desire to make the world a better place or all of the above!

Are they just plain stupid? No, they are intelligent people who are good at something (or think they are) who simply miss seeing all the other skills needed to start and run a business.

Our job? (Ta, Ta, Ta... Ta... Ta, Ta!) Is to save you from failure! At all cost! Well actually, at the cost of this book.

Seriously, our intent is to try and open your eyes to as many things as we can so that you stand a better chance at being successful in whatever business you choose to open.

Why are we qualified to give such advice? Because we have owned, co-owned and operated several businesses. We've worked in industries ranging from high tech to education to retail sales. We've traveled extensively, are well organized, most of the crayons are still in our boxes and we were both taught to apply common sense first to everything we do. We also were taught to be proactive, rather than reactive, a critical skill that seems to have been forgotten these days. The most compelling thing that qualifies us? We both love to teach and pass on our knowledge.

Much of what we will pass on are things we've learned from observing, asking the advice of others or from first-hand experience. Is what we cover a complete list of what you need to be successful in business? No. Will you need everything in this book? Probably not, even though we think everything we discuss will apply in one way or another.

Will you begin to ask more questions, jot down a list of things you need to do, list new skills you are going to need to develop or buy? We sincerely hope so because our sole intent is to make you realize the complete skill set you need to have available to make your business successful.

As you read, you'll see that we've divided our book into two parts: *Getting Your Business Started* and *The People Side of Things*. Also, you'll find we've divided skills into two major categories: Learned Skills and Intuitive Skills. Most of what is in Part 1 would likely fall under learned skills while the people part will deal with a lot of intuitive skills.

Wherever possible, we've tried to add examples to help clarify what we're talking about.

Finally, to top things off, in Part 3, you'll find some stories from our experience that we hope will offer some insight, help prepare you for the journey you're about to embark on and, in some cases, highlight the funnier side of business and bring a smile to your face.

At the end of each chapter you'll also find a short summary and an exercise to help you lose weight. Oops, sorry, to help you apply what we've covered in that chapter. These exercises are just guidelines so feel free to ignore them if you don't think they apply or modify them to fit your form of business.

So, You Want to Start Your Own Business

A quick story. (Ha, you'll learn nothing is quick with us, since we're both story tellers. But this does contain the most important message we could possibly give you.)

When Bob and his wife decided to open a restaurant back in the mid 1980s, they began by researching books written by restaurateurs that gave advice on how to open and successfully operate a restaurant. They quickly learned that many of them were poorly written but had an important message or two if you were patient enough to struggle through the "who cares" parts. Worse yet, much of the advice either didn't make sense (like, why would I ever do that?) or was so unique to the writer's situation that it had no value to them.

One book, however, was very well written and seemed to cover almost all the things they wanted to know about and answered many of the questions they had. It was written by a man who operated an extremely popular and successful dinner house in a small California coastal town. As fate would have it, his restaurant was also less than 30 miles from the front-running town they were considering for their restaurant.

During one of their many scouting trips to their target town, they decided to call him and see if he would meet with them and offer whatever advice he might be willing to share. He gladly agreed and asked only that they arrive between lunch and dinner hours, so he would have time to spend with them with as few interruptions as possible.

When they arrived, he sat them in a large booth and immediately asked two things: "Would you like me to autograph my book, and have you set aside money to start your restaurant?" They answered yes to both questions and he signed their copy of his book. He then said, "So you want to open your own restaurant? I will give you the best advice you will ever get. Take half of the money you have saved and burn it! Take the other half and go on vacation for as long as the money lasts. When you return, go to work for someone else and let them deal with all the problems! You'll be much better off!"

That turned out to truly be the best advice anyone could give about opening your own business. Did it discourage them? No, nor are we trying to discourage you. What it did do was open their eyes to the fact that this wasn't going to be a cake walk. They really needed to think about what they were doing.

The next four hours were spent with him sharing some of the most funny, rewarding and horrible experiences and stories they had ever heard. Just before they left, he looked at both of them and closed with, "I would not trade one minute of running this restaurant for anything in the world!"

Our point in telling this story is simple: To open your eyes and get you to strap in! Opening your own business is probably the hardest thing you'll ever do. It will probably take every cent you have set aside and then a bunch more. You'll likely devote most of your waking hours to making it work. You'll have to learn things you never knew about or wanted to know about. Decisions will keep you up night after night and it'll encroach on your personal life (if you let it) like nothing else ever will.

But if you stick with it and make it successful, it will likely be the most rewarding and exciting thing you'll ever do!

Who Should Read This Book?

The simple answer... everyone.

However, we've added the following list of diverse business types. In each case, you can apply what we'll cover in the various chapters to each business type. The point being; no matter what kind of business you're planning on, the steps we cover will apply. Some things may need to be tailored slightly or a lot for one business or another, but the elements to successfully establish and run a business are the same, no matter what your service or product is.

Lawn mowing	Book Store	Tree trimmer
Carpet cleaning	Pet store	Computer repair/help
Pest removal	Remodeling	Vege stand/market
Bicycle repair shop	Restaurants	Carpentry
Car yards/sales	Bars/pubs	Pet grooming
Bungy jumping	Fast food/franchises	Catering
Travel agent	Food Truck	Author/writer
Coffee shop	Craft Sales	Gardener
Aromatherapist	Garden Center	Vending machines
Oven cleaners	Clairvoyant	Ice Cream Truck
Private tuition	Wine shop	Marijuana sales
Website design	Mobile Drinks van	Handyman
Hairdressers	Electrician	Self-serve cut flowers
Limo services	Plumber	Brothel
Sea, surf, dive	Rental Property	Wine Bar
Pet/house sitters	Apartment building	Heating/Air Conditioning

Part 1- Getting Your Business Started

Chapter 1 – Basic Elements

The three most important elements to any business are:

Research
A Sound Business Plan
Location

We'll cover these in depth in upcoming chapters, but not in the above order. We've put research first because it's not only the most important thing you'll do but the thing you do most as you build your business plan and determining the location that will best suit your business.

In the meantime, let's start with a few quick definitions. We'll keep these as short as possible but, believe us, if they weren't important we wouldn't put them right up front.

Learned Skills

For the sake of discussion, we've divided the business skills you might need into two categories: Learned skills and Intuitive skills.

Learned skills are those business skills that will apply to almost any business in one form or another. They may be learned by you (e.g. you could go to school to learn how to mix drinks for your bar or how to keep your books) or you could purchase them, (e.g. you might choose to hire a trained bartender or contract out your bookkeeping to an accountant or firm.)

Pretty simple, huh? Not quite as simple as it might seem. As you go through each section, pay particular attention to where we talk about skills that are typically hired out.

Why? Just because you hire someone to do something, doesn't mean you don't need to know anything about it. As a matter of fact, quite the opposite.

First, you'll need to know enough to be able to assess someone's skills and experience when you're interviewing or deciding who to contract them out to. Not just the skills and experience they have but whether those skills apply directly to the needs of your business.

Second, if you do hire them, you'll need to oversee and evaluate what they're doing. You're putting a part (in some cases a major part) of your business and its success or failure, in their hands. So you need to know what they're doing! That goes for the dish washer, the janitor, the manager, or the accountant. The minute you hire them, they **are** your business!

Intuitive skills

Intuitive skills are things that you feel. Things that are based on your instincts or that **you** reason to be true. They're the things that your gut instinct tells you, often without proof or logic.

Are they important? You bet. They are often the thing that will determine success or failure.

Let us give you an example.

Part of Bob's job as a volunteer at the San Diego Zoo is to mentor new volunteers. Before he gets to mentor them, each volunteer is required to spend hours doing on-line training to learn about the animals they'll be talking to guests about. After their on-line training, they spend a full day or two in classroom training at the zoo then get turned over to him.

Why? So he can teach them about the animals? Nope. It's now up to him to teach them the intuitive skills they'll need to be successful. How to come up with grab lines (words or comments) to attract people to their station. How to read the guests' eyes and body language to know whether or not they're holding their guests' interest and, if not, how to change gears.

In short, all their knowledge about the animals won't accomplish anything if they can't gain and hold the interest of their audience. Thus their success or failure depends as much or more on their intuitive skills as it does their learned skills.

Likewise, Robyn uses the same techniques when teaching students. Constantly noting whether they're paying attention or if they've drifted elsewhere is critical to her getting her messages across. And her classes being praised so she can attract new business.

Not all skills you'll need will fit neatly into one category or the other. But it's the skill, not where it fits, that we care about.

Success

Let's take a minute and talk about success. The intent of the upcoming outline and business plan is to help move your business from an idea to a concept, and hopefully, push you and it into the "real world". Having done that, we can go on to setting some realistic goals that will then **allow you** to define success.

We cannot emphasize this enough:

Success (and failure) are what you define them to be

They aren't what your family, friends, customers, books on owning a business or anyone else think they are.

Failure

Let's jump over to failure.

(This will seem a bit long and rambly so we're going to ask you to hang in there. Trust us, it'll be worth it and it contains some very important messages.)

What if you don't meet your goals? OMG, you're such a complete failure! You fail and you become a worthless piece of crap! No one will ever love you again! Your family will disown you! You will be shunned on the street! Worse of all, you will be "Unliked" on Facebook and people will tweet about what a lowly turd you are!

Ridiculous, right? Not really. One thing that comes with owning your own business is easily losing track of what's real and what's not and often what's important and what's not.

When you devote everything to making something work and it (or some part of it) doesn't, it can be devastating. The key is to not let that happen by putting the right perspective on everything and not letting your emotions overrule logic.

Remember, you're the one who defines success and failure so let's start with that.

First of all, failure is NOT BAD! As Bram Stoker wrote in Dracula, "We learn from failure, not from success!" Failure is how we learn. It's how we discover issues and areas we were never exposed to before. So let's think of failure as a "discovery and learning opportunity" rather than having not accomplished something.

Damage Control

There's another critically important element to this though. To feel good about our failures and turn them into learning experiences, we need to minimize any harm they might cause. Whenever we run into something we're not sure of, have never done before or that may not work, we're going to try and do three things:

> First, put the right perspective on what we want to do and assess how important it is in the whole scheme of things.

> Second, if it's really important to our overall success, we're going to try to intelligently divide it up into as many smaller issues as we can to help reach a resolution.

Emotion

> Third, try and separate (or at least identify) emotion when it plays a role or drives decisions.

Here's an example to help illustrate this:

Two young women (Daisy Mist and Grazilla) who grew up together, love to play soccer and their dream has always been to own a sports bar. They're now the proud owners of Mecca's Bar, a bar with a Mexican flare! (OLE!) They purchased this well run, profitable bar from a widow (Maria Estella Carman Chiquita Augustine aka Mecca) who

24

moved to Florida to sell crab tacos from a beach stand in Fort Lauderdale.

Mecca left them with everything they needed to be successful: a great staff, a plethora of happy, longtime customers, her recipes for great tropical style drinks and a set of books defining everything they needed to know and do to keep the business running smoothly.

Are they happy campers or what? But wait, one month into this and they realize this isn't working. This isn't "their dream bar"; it's Mecca's. They need to put their own flare on it and make it into the bar they envisioned so they can do all the things they'd planned.

But Mecca was Mexican, the whole ambience is Mexican and the drink theme is Tropical. And the name "Mecca's Bar" - EEW! That's gotta go.

The solution? Simple, change it into a soccer sports bar. ASAP!

Now there are two ways the girls can do this. Close for a few days, jump in and change everything needed to make it into their dream soccer bar. Or step back and assess the potential impact of each of the changes they would like to make before they decide how (or even if) they want to make the change.

First, overall, is this a major change? You bet. Every customer coming through the door expects to see Mexican décor and sip drinks with umbrellas hanging out of them. If customers don't want a soccer bar or like sporty drinks, the girls are going to lose their established customer base.

Is this change important? You bet. They need to fulfill their dream and put all the ideas they have into **their place**. Is there emotion involved? (Do we really need to go there?)

So let's see if they can divide this change up, evaluate it and minimize the risk so their dream bar doesn't become a bust.

The girls start by looking at what they want to change and roughly how hard each part of the change will be.

Redecorating will be easy: replace the several hundred sombreros hanging everywhere with sports stuff. Add several big screen TVs (not so easy). Change the drinks by replacing the umbrellas with little lacrosse sticks and add more beers. Easy.

Change the name! WOW, we need a new name! "Daisy Mist and Grazilla's Place"? Not a good name for a sports bar, sounds more like a vampire hangout! (You knew Bob would work vampires into this somehow!)

The girls quickly realize that even the easy changes are going to require some thought. So they decide to try to learn what their customers would like in order to decide which changes might work and which might not.

They start with a little investigation:

- Are there any sports bars nearby?
- If so, will they be competing with them?
- Do they want to compete with them?
- What would their customers think of a sports bar? Why not ask them?

- Have they considered all of the parts to the change and how much will each part of the change cost to implement?
- What impact will the change have on their operating costs?

If the answers to these questions are favorable then they can look at how they want to change the theme: Overnight or phase it in and, do they have a choice?

What about the name? That's gotta go: Pronto!

In this way, the girls are looking at not only how will the customers accept the change but which parts of the change will be the hardest, most costly and have the highest risk.

They can further divide the high risk areas into several steps, each of which has a much smaller risk. Each smaller step, if it fails, will hopefully have minimal impact on the success of their business, help them learn if their customers will accept the change or, if need be, try a different approach.

As so often happens, at this point Daisy Mist looks wide eyed at Grazilla and smacks her forehead (her own forehead). "OMG! We're so stupid! Where have our heads been?" (Daisy Mist is obviously having an A-ha moment.)

"They love soccer in Mexico! Why don't we keep the Mexican theme, modify it toward soccer and other sports and keep all of our customers?

"And! And! What if we change the name to The Sports Mecca? That way we're not really changing the name and can keep name recognition!" (You go girl!)

Daisy Mist and Grazilla now own the most profitable sports bar in town, vacation monthly in Fort Lauderdale and are Mecca's best customers for crab tacos!

So what have we done? We've tried to point out several things in this example (aside from our story telling talent):

1. The girls wisely bought an established, well run concern that really didn't need any changes.

2. They put the right perspective on what they wanted to do. They realized emotion played a large part in their decision to change the bar's theme but still considered it important to them.

3. They realized the change wasn't simple and could have a major impact on their successfully running business.

4. They divided the change up into a series of smaller changes to evaluate the impact of each and determined the best way to implement the pieces to minimize risk.

5. Finally, in the course of exploring their options, they came up with a way to realize their dream, minimalize the changes and keep their customers happy.

By doing all this, they assured that their failures (if any) would have as minor an impact as possible on the success of their business. More importantly, as often happens, dividing up their change allowed them to analyze each piece, better understand its impact and come up with solutions that greatly reduced their risk of failure.

Summary

In this chapter, we have tried to define some of the basic elements you'll need to understand and use to help you build a successful business.

Most importantly, we defined success and failure in a different light.

Success and failure are what you define them to be

Failure is NOT BAD - We learn from failure, more than from success

In the examples, we've tried to point out how we all have failures and successes as we go through life. How they play an important part in how we learn new things. How they provide incentive for us to do better, grow and move up to the next level. How they help us set new goals and measure our progress toward meeting them. How they boost our confidence and pride when we achieve what we set out to do.

And that often our perceived failures are not failures at all. They are simply things that didn't come out the way we wanted them to.

As the saying goes: "It takes a hundred atta-boys to erase one ah-shit!" But we guarantee you will remember the ah-shit long after memories of the atta-boys have faded away. Likewise, one failure may offset a lot of wins, but you'll learn so much more from that one failure. To be successful in business the key is to **minimize the effect** of the ah-shits and failures while **maximizing the lessons** you take away from them.

We also introduced emotion. How our business is our dream and because of that, it is easy to get totally wrapped up in our ideas. This cannot only blind you to the impact and risk of doing something but prevent you from recognizing and considering other options. And how to make you aware of the role emotion will play in your decisions, how to recognize it and do damage control when something doesn't work.

Exercise

1. List what you define as your business being successful. (Let's stay at a high level for right now. We'll add the fine details later as we expand things.)
2. List what you would consider to be failures. Next to each, add what you think you would learn from it and what type of damage control you could use to minimize any impact.
3. List as best you can, areas where you think emotion is going to play a part in your business and what you consider success or failure.
4. Identify things you think you're going to need to research and possible sources for doing that research.

Remember, we're at a pretty high level here so try not to get too deep yet. The whole purpose of this exercise is to get you to start thinking about each of the elements as they might apply to your business. The details will come later.

Uh... Yes, we skipped skills. Nice catch! Not to worry though, we'll talk about skills in almost every chapter from here on out.

Notes

Chapter 2 - How to Get Started

A lot of what we tell you will simply be common business sense. But most of us aren't born with common business sense so we guarantee that you'll sit back at some point and say, "Crap, I never thought of that!" If (when) that happens we'll be happy campers because we've added some value to you starting your own business and hopefully helped to make it a success.

If you go, "Crap, I knew that!" for everything? You need to write your own book.

Let's begin with: what is the business you want to start? What is it really? At first many of us don't know what specific business we want to have or will end up with. We simply start with an idea or concept.

"I want to make the world a better place!" Great, but how? Do you want to invent something to make it better? Sell something to make it better? Tell people how to make it better? What exactly is it you want to do? More importantly, what do **you want the business to do**?

Your Concept

We suggest you start by writing out your concept; the general notion and ideas of whatever it is you think your business will be.

Do you want to do construction? What kind of construction? Business, residential, new homes, new businesses, rehab, renovation etc.

Do you want to sell door knobs? Fine, just door knobs? In a store? Door to door?

Don't be surprised if your answers come back, "I don't know" or you can't clearly state what you or your business will do. But if you don't define it, then how is anyone else supposed to know? So we need to narrow down what you want to do, for ourselves and our customers.

This may sound pretty stupid, but Bob has run into more than one person in the construction business who he's asked, "What do you do or specialize in?" and their response was either, "I'm good at everything" or "I'll do whatever you want me to do." Now seriously, are we going to hire that person? Not on your life!

Along the same lines, both Bob and Robyn have walked into stores or restaurants and after a few minutes of looking around or studying the menu wondered what kind of products they sold or food they specialized in. In many cases they tried to have something for everyone and ended up appealing to no one. These were the places they left promising to remember them... so they could be sure not to return.

You simply cannot be everything to everybody. Even if you are a J C Penny's or Walmart wannabe, you have to define and limit your market segment so you can zero in on that market. Especially when you first start out and need to get to light speed on so many new things.

The Start of Your Business Plan

Let's start to define what it is you want your business to do by developing a plan.

Our goal is to start out simple then grow it into a complete, top down plan. From this we'll likely generate several action plans that you'll use to define what you need to do to successfully launch and run your business.

If you're going to sell cupcakes or open an animal preserve, you're in luck as these are the examples we'll be using. Please feel free to use our plan and make it your own as much as you can as a guide. (This is your business, not ours and if you fail it's not our fault, cupcake!)

Example 1

You want to make cupcakes, great!

Let's start by exploring some of your ideas.

- Do you want to make them at home?
- Make them in someone else's kitchen?
- Rent a store front with a kitchen?
- Sell them from home on the curb?
- From the Internet?
- In bars and restaurants?

These are all questions that will come up as we develop the plan. This is a good thing! The whole purpose of the plan is to make you think!

The plan will really make you ask yourself, "Do I really want to do this?" If the answer comes back "NO" get your lighter and half of your savings out and start making vacation plans.

If the answer is "YES", let's start:

My Cupcake Business Plan (How original!)

At this point let's still keep the plan at a pretty high level. The plan will expand as questions are raised and the details will follow as you answer the questions.

Business Goal: Make and sell cupcakes
Where: Hicksville, NY

How: Bake cupcakes at: Home (expand to
store ASAP)
Sell To: Stores, Internet and out of house
Customers: Young people

So far, so good. I know this seems like DUH stuff but bear
with us. Let's go to the next level. We're still just getting
your ideas on paper and testing the water on how sound
they are, what you already know or what research you'll
need to do.

1. Goal: Make and sell cupcakes
   a. Type of cupcakes: My recipes only (custom,
      customer request?)

2. Where: Hicksville, NY

3. Bake Cupcakes at: Home (expand to store ASAP)
   a. Kitchen needs: Big enough? Equipment?
      Sanitary stuff?
   b. Store needs: ?????

4. Sell To: Stores, Internet and out of house
   a. Stores: Delis, mom/pop, bars
   b. In front of house (lemonade stand)
   c. Internet, Facebook friends

5. Customers: Young people
   a. Age group: 10-30
   b. Young people in Hicksville? How many,
      where?

As your plan expands, the following types of questions
should be rattling around in the back of your head:

- Can you make custom or customer requested
  cupcakes or only ones from your recipes?
- Can you even make cupcakes or do you just think
  you can make them?
- Is Hicksville a good place for this type of business?

- Do any young people live there or is it a retirement community?
- Maybe you need to move or make "old people cupcakes" and sell them at retirement homes.
- Are there any deli's or mom and pop stores there, with old people hanging around out front?
- Will my three Facebook friends really buy my cupcakes? Will they "Like" me on Facebook? What if they "Unlike me"? OMG! My business is screwed and I haven't even made my first cupcake yet! Where's my lighter?

Example 2

Okay, so screw the cupcake business and let's open a Wild Animal Preserve and save all of the endangered animals in the world! Yay! Go PETA!

Business Goal: Save animals. Open and run an animal preserve
Where: Podunk, San Diego County, CA
Product: Animals?
Sell: Nothing (???)
Customers: Animal Lovers

Taking this to the next level.

1. Goals:
    a. Save animals
        i. What type of animals need saving?
        ii. Do they live around here?
        iii. Save from what, who and how?
    b. Open and run an animal preserve
        i. What's an animal preserve?
        ii. Will they come if I open it?

2. Where: Podunk, San Diego County, CA
    a. Is Podunk a good place?

36

b. Are there animals in Podunk that need saving or do I need to import them?

c. If not Podunk, what's close?

3. What do I need to make a preserve?
    a. Land – How much?
    b. People – How many? Skills?
    c. OMG! I'm going to need a vet!

4. Product: Animals (Do I really have a product?)
    a. Shelter
    b. Love
    c. Caring

5. Sell: Nothing (???)
    a. Concern for animals
    b. Education
    c. Impact on future generations
    d. Sympathy (so I can collect donations)

6. Customers:
    a. Animal lovers
    b. Animal rights groups
    c. Zoo people

I hope what we're trying to do is beginning to sink in. (If not, we're screwed and need to go back to writing romance novels or switch to writing vampire novels, which is actually next up on Bob's bucket list.)

The plan doesn't have to be in outline form and there is no right or wrong way to do the plan. It is strictly what YOU want it to be, what works for YOU. These are your ideas, expanding as YOU think of what comes next.

Our job is to get the old gears moving and make you think about how you are going to pull this off. There is no right or wrong!

As you expand your plan use common and business sense. What comes next? Key off words in the category to help expand it. What's missing? Did you leave part of something out?

Not sure? Look it up. Remember, **research, research, research.**

Anything is fair game, especially at this point. Jot down anything and everything that comes to you no matter how crazy it might be and stick it somewhere. You can always delete or move it later to where it may make more sense but, for now, get it down somewhere, anywhere. There is no right or wrong!

Stop when you:

> Think you're done
> Run out of ideas
> Things are not really making sense any more
> Decide this is not working
> Need to make a beer or wine run

Set the plan aside for a minute and clear your head. If you're like us, you now have a thousand ideas running around in your head and will be picking up the plan every few minutes to add something to it.

Summary

So far we've talked a lot and hopefully you've listened. Our main goal in this chapter was simply to get the gears moving, have you start a business plan, and get you thinking about what it is you want your business to do or provide, and to who.

Exercise

Create a top level business plan by filling in the following:

1. Your business goal: What do you envision your business being?
    a. Expand by jotting down as many details as you wish.

2. Where: Where do you think you want to open it?
    a. Alternate locations to consider?
    b. Research needed for each location?

3. Product(s): What product(s) and/or services will you sell?
    a. Expand with as many products or services as you think you want or need to provide.

4. Sell To: Who are you going to sell to and how?
    a. Retail/wholesale.
    b. Brick and mortar business.
    c. Internet business.

5. Customers: Who will be your customers?
    a. Age, ethnicity, income, other factors you want/need to appeal to?

Notes

Chapter 3 – Making Your Business Plan Real

Restating Your Goals

Now that you have surrounded your business idea with a bit of reality, let's go back and look at the business goal(s) in your plan. Remember, we've moved into the real world now so try keep things definable, real and achievable. Also, make sure they are yours. At this point we suggest you still keep them simple. You can always expand on them or completely change them as you go.

Example 1 - Cupcakes

Do you really want to "Make and sell cupcakes"?

How about "Make and sell cupcakes for a profit"?

Let's try this:

"Make and sell the best cupcakes in town and make a profit you can live off."

Example 2 - Save the animals

Do you want to "Save animals? Open and run an animal preserve"?

How about "Open an animal preserve that saves all animals"?

Kind of hard to save all animals, but since you love horses how about: "Open an animal preserve that saves horses"?

Let's try:

"Open a ranch that takes in and cares for abandoned horses?"

In one case we simply expanded upon the original goal. In the other we pretty much redefined the goal to what we likely had in mind in the first place and made it more realistic.

Why are we even bringing this up? Because we want you to be successful and to be successful you need to set realistic goals that you can achieve.

Being everything to everybody, saving all the world's animals, curing all the world's problems on the first day you open is not achievable. Be one thing to one person, save one animal or cure one world problem, then bump your goals up and expand your business to do more.

If you open your cupcake stand, sell a dozen cupcakes each day and live happily ever after on the profit, you're successful.

If you open a horse ranch and save one abandoned horse you've been successful.

Are you going to stop there? No, but you have an achievable goal, you feel good about yourself, your business ideas are working and you can start planning your next step.

Research

In the previous sections, we hope that the examples and exercises you've done have made you aware of at least a few things you didn't realize and need to look into: things you need to research and things you didn't even know you didn't know.

Throughout our book you will find us reiterating a number of things. One of these would be: **Research, research, research**!

Research is very important. Why? Because you can't know everything about starting a business. Research doesn't have to be in depth; it can be as little or as much as you want or need it to be. You need to be able to have done enough research to be able to define and refine your business ideas, decide what you want to do, learn more about or hire and contract out for things you don't want to take on.

Defining Your Business

Let's get back to your plan and see if we can start to really define your business by adding the "What, where, how and who".

- What you want to do.
- Where you want to (or need to) do it.
- How you plan to do it.
- Who you want to do it to (or for).

This will form a solid base to start from. From there you'll expand your business ideas and develop action and research plans or lists.

Exercise

This whole chapter is basically an exercise, as will a lot of the upcoming chapters. At the end, we'll summarize what your plan should contain.

What You Want to do

If you're happy with your goals, you now need to figure out how you're going to accomplish them. If you think your goals are incomplete you can either try to expand on them or wait and see what falls out as we progress.

What Are You Going to Sell or Provide?

List what it is you want to sell or provide. This can be a product or collection of products. It can be a service or, most likely, it will be a combination of products and services.

The division may not always be clear so here are a few examples.

Door knobs

If you sell door knobs on the Internet but offer nothing else in the way of support services, you're selling a product. If you sell door knobs on the Internet but also offer advice on how to select the proper door knob, provide installation instructions and offer answers to customer questions via email, you are selling products and providing related services.

Cupcakes

If you sell cupcakes from a lemonade stand in front of your house, you're selling a product. If you sell those same cupcakes from a store front, offer to deliver them or serve them at tables on the patio in front of the store, you're selling a product and providing services.

Abandoned Horses

If you run a ranch that takes in and cares for abandoned horses you're providing a service. This assumes you aren't selling the horses because:

a.   You really don't own them.
b.   They're not able to work or be ridden, and

c.   You fall in love with them as soon as they come through the gate and wouldn't dream of selling them. (Yes, we support and are good friends with someone who owns a ranch that takes in abandoned horses.)

Restaurant

If you own a restaurant, you sell food and provide services. Notice that we said you sell food and not meals. Why? Because more often than not the food is cooked to request and the guest ordering the food selects what side dishes they would like. So in truth, you are providing a series of services including cooking the food to order, building a meal to order and serving it to the guest.

Okay. So why are we being such a pain in the ass about this? Because we really want you to think about what your business actually is. Most people who open a restaurant do so because they love to cook or love eating good food. But when you own a restaurant, cooking good food will be the least of your worries. In fact, you're providing a whole bunch of services and how well you provide those services is going to weigh heavily on your success and how people rate your business.

Where Are You Going to Provide it?

Now that you think you know what products and services your business will provide, we can look at where you think you want to provide it.

Let's start by making a list of potential locations:

- Hicksville for your cupcake stand.
- Podunk for your horse ranch.
- Cape Town for your vampire accessory store.

List your primary location first and then try and come up with as many alternate locations as you can. Why? Because we are going to use this list to evaluate each location and see if:

a. It is ideal (or close to it) for your type of business.
b. It has the physical elements you need to start and keep your business running successfully, and
c. It has the support elements available that you might need.

Confused? How about another example to help you understand how our minds work (or, as we refer to them: The Scary Places!).

Let's say you want to open a hair salon and you live in Prairie View, Texas. Obviously, Prairie View will be first on your list. Now let's look at other places nearby that you think would be close enough and acceptable alternatives. That might give you a list something like:

- Prairie View

- Hempstead

- Chappell Hill

- Waller

- Hockley

(Yes, these really do exist and are actually great little towns between Houston and Austin, Texas.)

As we get further into our plan we're going to start bouncing things off our primary location to make sure it's a good fit.

For example:

- What is the population of Prairie View and the surrounding areas?
- Is it big enough to support a hair salon?

- Are there any other hair salons there? If so how many?
- Where would be a good place in town for a hair salon?
- Are there store fronts available there?
- You'll likely need other hairdressers; are there any there?
- You'll need a hair salon supply store, is there one close by?

If the answer to some or all of these questions eliminates our primary location then we will need to look at one or more of our alternatives until we find the ideal (or close to it) location.

Anyone who has been to Prairie View pretty much knows it would work well for a hair salon location with:

- A good size population.
- High school and college in town, and
- Most of the other elements there or close by.

But, you know what? It still doesn't hurt to run through this exercise just to be sure you've covered all the bases. The more you make sure you have everything you could possibly need the better your chances of success. More importantly, the better you understand your business and its environment, the better prepared you'll be for the unexpected, keeping it fresh or expanding it in the future.

Since we're still at the 1,000 foot level, let's not eliminate anything yet. Unless it's obviously not going to work at all like selling pork pies in a predominately Jewish neighborhood or styling Afros in a retirement home where everyone has little to no hair. If a place is looking like it might not work simply note why and keep going. If you listed it, you must have had a reason and we'll come back later and see if we might be able to make it work. (Hopefully, you'll see what we mean as we go.)

A special note to those of you who are thinking of providing goods and services through the Internet

At first glance you might be saying none of this applies to me. However, you might want to take another look.

- Are you going to be shipping stuff?
- Is your business completely dependent on staying on-line?
- If you live in the boondocks is there anybody nearby to ship your stuff?
- Is there a place for receiving and storing your inventory?
- Is power reliable in the area?
- Is high speed internet service, sufficient for your business, available?
- Do you have computer support services close by in case you need them?

Losing power for a day or two or having your computer hacked is extremely annoying when it interferes with your personal life. When your computer being on-line is critical to your business and future income, being hacked or losing power takes on a whole different meaning!

How Are You Going to Provide it?

Now that we think we know the where, let's look at the how.

- Is the business to operate out of your home?
- From a store front?
- On the Internet? Or
- Is it going to be a combination of these?

You also might want to think about the future. Do you plan on starting one way, expand to operate from more than one location or move it completely?

For example, we can operate our hair salon from the back porch or laundry room of our home to start with. Once we've established a customer base, we can look at moving it to a store front.

Our friend in Hicksville thought about selling cupcakes from a stand in front of their house as well as in local bars and mom and pop stores. But they might want to branch to a storefront and/or Internet sales as business picks up.

Our horsey person is going to be pretty much limited to a ranch or a VERY BIG back yard! However, will their ranch be big enough as they accumulate more and more horses?

We know this is going to sound completely stupid but as your "How list" comes together, really think about if each "How" is going to work.

- Is selling cupcakes as bar food in a bar going to work?
- When you live in Hicksville, NY is a sidewalk stand in front of your house a good place to sell anything from in the winter?
- Is trying to start a home for abandoned horses from your back yard really a good idea? (NIMBY - Not in my back yard, you don't.)

Please understand! We're in no way trying to discourage you! We're just trying to get you to think things through! Sometimes an obvious "No way" can become a "Way" if we just think a little outside the box.

Sell cupcakes in a bar? A young lady in San Diego sells specialty cupcakes made with beer in several bars and does quite well.

In addition to styling Afros you might also stumble upon an opportunity to wash and trim wigs at that retirement home full of bald people.

As for selling pork pies in a Jewish neighborhood, there is no hope for you or your business. You have failed miserably and we suggest you seriously look into cupcakes!

Who Are You Going to Provide it to?

Oh God, aren't we done yet? Nope! We have lofty goals, fantastic products and outstanding services, a superb location and an ingenious way to peddle our wares. But just who are we going to peddle this stuff to?

Every product (or service) has a target market:

- Toys to kids.
- Italian food to Italians.
- Dresses to woman.
- Food to people looking for something to eat.
- Hairstyles to people with hair.
- Mouthwash to people with bad breath.
- Pooper scoopers to people with dogs.
- Little pooper scoopers to people with cats.
- Mittens to people with hands.

Seriously, take a good look at everything we've listed. Are they real? Kinda? What they are is very limited. Do you only want to sell your Italian food to Italians? Do most kids buy their own toys? How about their parents? Do people only buy mouthwash because they have bad breath? The pooper scooper market is pretty much locked into people with pets (or little kids. Eew!)

Our point? So many of us unintentionally limit our market to only the obvious. We target only the center and miss the fringe markets. Think carefully about who makes up your market. Have you included those just outside? Who else would you like to target? What do you need to do to sell your stuff to them?

Try and list everything and everyone that might even be remotely interested in what you're selling or doing, e.g:

- What about other businesses?
- What about selling your cupcakes to coffee shops?
- What about styling wigs at retirement homes, or hospitals with cancer patients?
- How about volunteering at the horse preserve so you can save a life while you let people know you're a damn good vet who cares?

WOW, we don't know about you but we're just about wiped out! This is really hard work!

Yes it is, but we've been here before and believe us it will all pay off. Before Bob and his wife opened the restaurant they did over two years of demographic research to find a location and tried to plan out the business every which way from Sunday. With his remodeling business, it took him over ten years before he felt comfortable opening it.

Before starting her businesses, Robyn took a year to research who else was providing secretarial services specializing in minute taking and when she began her training business, what other organisations were providing administration training.

Did we do everything we've told you to do? Hell no! We weren't that smart back then. But we are now and hope we've learned enough to pass it on to you. Why? Because we love helping people and the further we get into this book the more things we think of, the more friends we ask for help and the more excited we get.

Were we successful in our businesses? We think we were. And really, that's all that counts!

Summary

By now you should have a top level business plan with the following:

- Your business products and services (what you want to do).
- Your potential location, location, location (where you want or need to do it).
- Your business type: Store front, Internet, other (how you plan to do it), and
- Your customers (who you want to do it to, or for).

Next to that, or included, should be dozens and dozens of questions, answers and other gibberish that we will try to sort out, define and expand upon in the remaining chapters.

Exercise (Continued)

From here on out, you're on your own! Well, kinda. We're going to give you a pat on the head and slight push on the butt and send you into the cold, cruel world to finish expanding your business plan! (Oh no! They hate me! I've failed again and am nothing but cow poo! Why? Why are you abandoning me now?)

Mostly because we can't think of anything else **we can add** to the plan that will help you. Are we out of stuff to talk about? Never! As our friends (all three of them) will assure you.

If you've not spent the last few hours finalizing your vacation plans and packing, we hope you've been feverishly adding to and developing your business plan.

What is covered next will be a series of things that should apply to every business, but don't necessarily fit neatly into your business plan. Where you put them or how you fit them in is up to you. (Wow! They do trust me! I'm really not cow poo! Yet!)

You may have noticed us wandering around and some things not quite fitting where we put them. That's because some things can apply to several areas or not fit neatly into any particular one. So if you think it fits somewhere else in your business plan, great, move it! You may also think of something we did not. That is really great because it says you're doing exactly what you should be doing: taking the reins of your business plan and running with it. To repeat, we can't cover everything. But we do hope we've laid down a basic framework for your plan and gotten the old gears to start turning.

Notes

Chapter 4 - Your Business as Others See It

The Name Game

Now that we know what YOU want your business to be, what do you want others to see it as? What Identity do you envision? What image do you want others to see?

You may not have thought about it but names, symbols, locations and even colors can conger up an image or association that you may or may not be looking for.

More than likely one of the first things you thought of was a name for your business, probably before you even knew what your business was going to be! (Are we good or what? Great! Now they're going to pick on the totally unique, cutesy name that took me hours to come up with!)

If you haven't picked a name yet, you need to do it in this section. Seriously, as you'll see in many of the following chapters, you'll not get very far without a business name.

So let's help you pick a name. Or, if you already have one, let's make sure it fits and serves your business well.

Many of us see a name or title and immediately associate it with something. These associations can either be conscious or subconscious. Gee, do you think maybe the marketing companies had anything to do with that? If the name, title, or words you use in describing your business have an association, you need to be very aware of it.

For example: When Bob sees a place named "Jonny's" he immediately thinks of a 50s or 60s themed drive in with girls on roller skates buzzing around the parking lot with trays held high in one hand. Why? He has no idea. He doesn't ever remember being in a "Jonny's" drive-in. Maybe he saw it on a TV show or in an ad but that's the image that pops into his mind. Okay, so he's weird! By now you've figured that out. But he's not the only weird person in this world and he's certainly not the only one who sees "Jonny's" and thinks "Drive-In"! (Is he?)

Robyn's too young to remember the 50s, 60s and drive-ins but, in Blenheim there is a café with a great name called the Watery Mouth. It's pretty obvious what will be drunk at The Vines and what kind of food do you think might be served at The Good Home?

Okay, let's try some others.

Jose or Carlotta says Mexican.
Amelie says girl next door wearing a sweater and pearls.
Rose says beautiful, sweet smelling and red.
Daisy says light, airy and bright yellow.
Sargent says policeman or soldier.
San Diego and Blenheim, New Zealand says sun, beaches, fun.
Denny's says breakfast.
O'Hara says Irish.
Giovanni says Italian.
Mr adds a touch of class or elegance.
Grazilla says? (We're not sure what Grazilla says! Fangs? Sorry Grazilla!)

Let's Move on to Symbols

A rainbow arch is associated with gay pride.
Two split fingers can mean peace or victory (and other things).
The middle finger means (well, we all know what it means).
The coke bottle outline means Coca-Cola.
An arrow through a heart means love.
A sleigh being towed by reindeer means Santa or Christmas.
The Star of David or a Menorah means Jewish or Kosher.

How About Phrases or Words

Italian restaurant equals spaghetti and meatballs, and lasagna.

Mediterranean food equals light, cooked in olive oil.

New York pizza equals The World's Best Pizza! (Yes, Bob's originally from New York).

Family owned, (family run) means warm, friendly, inviting.

Under New Ownership means we changed everything you didn't like. (We hope!)

Casual, means laid back, comfortable, informal.

Note: Isn't it funny that Italy is in the Mediterranean yet, Italian and Mediterranean each brings up a very different image?

We can go on and on with old, new, modern, casual, hippy, mod, cheap, upper class, white, Latino, Afro-American, southern style... each of which probably creates at least a slightly different image for everyone reading this.

Many of these images or associations may be racial, regional, age related or just plain foreign to you. Others will vary with a person's background, who they grew up with, where and when they grew up, religion and family traditions. All of which says, you can't possibly be aware of hundreds of these associations.

Great, so once again, what's our point?

Research! Research! Research!

Once you decide on a name, a slogan or anything else related to your business that you're going to publicly display, you need to do your best to make sure it conveys the image you want. You also want to make sure it doesn't unintentionally insult anyone or make a statement you don't intend to make.

This is one time where the Internet can be of major benefit. Google your business name or slogan and see what pops up. Hang onto your chair when you do. You may be very surprised at what comes back! If a porn website shows up you should seriously think about a new name for your business! But don't just stop at the first page of Google results. Often the surprises might be buried two-three pages in.

Opening a restaurant or bar and you creatively named your dishes and drinks? Google them! Better to find out now that the stew you named Ranchipur Zozo actually means Ranchipur's Big Penis in African Creole. Or that your best selling bar drink, the Tembo Tatti, comes out pachyderm poop in Punjab! (Sorry guys, Tambo and Ranchipur are two elephants at the San Diego Zoo. And, actually, Tembo is a girl.)

Likewise, make sure you know the meaning of all the symbols you use. If you name your business "The Numero Uno Pizza Parlor" we would seriously suggest you **not** use a hand with the middle finger extended above the words Pizza Parlor as your business symbol! Or a heart with an arrow through it won't likely get the right message across if you're an undertaker.

Note: Our apologies to Tembo and Ranchipur, we didn't mean to insult them. On the contrary, we're trying to prevent you from accidently or unintentionally insulting someone! If you haven't been out in the world much, it's so easy to accidently offend someone! Use the Internet, run things by your friends and people with a variety of backgrounds. Anything you can do to try and make sure what you say or display in public is acceptable and not offensive.

One more example. When Robyn was walking back from breakfast on a training trip to Rotorua she passed a small architecture business called Stiffe Hooker. We don't think we need to add anything here other than they obviously didn't do much research or deliberately wanted to see how much attention they could attract.

Location, Location, Location

There are (or should be) many factors that drive the location you pick for your business. Cost, availability or both are usually the most common deciding factors. Cheap rents, available store fronts that already have the equipment you need installed or local zoning ordinances many times force a business to end up in a not so ideal location.

This is why we've implied several times that you may not end up where you originally planned. Then too, where you originally planned may not be where you truly want to end up. (Remember Hicksville and the old people?)

The key to selecting a location is **research, research, research**. Even if you can end up in your ideal location you're going to need to know where plan B, plan C and plan D would take you.

Since both Bob and Robyn are list people, start by listing what you think is:

- Critical
- Very important
- Important, and

- Not so important

about location to your business. Then try to hone in on each area for key things you need to look for.

Start with what you're selling and who you're selling it to. If your business is to be a bar or restaurant you'll need a store front (or something similar). Selling stuff on the Internet? You'll need a place to store and ship things from your basement or a warehouse. Does your product appeal to kids, young people, middle aged people, older people or all of the above? Are you going to sell stuff to business? If so, what kind of business?

Some key things to consider:

- Market segment?
- Neighborhood type?
- Age Group?
- Blue/white collar appeal?
- Race?
- Nationality?
- Business/residential?
- Income level?
- Businesses close by?
- Facilities you'll need close by (shipping, packaging, etc).

Where are we headed? Want to sell unusual antiques or open a restaurant with unusual menu items? Then you'll want to look for eclectic neighborhoods where high income yuppies live.

Want to open a funeral home? Looking for an area with retirement homes or communities close by would be a good start.

Let's try a more concrete example. You want to open a health food store that sells only healthy stuff. (Bob started writing this part but to him steak, sausage and beer are health foods. So Robyn took over.)

Examples

You want to sell only locally grown organic produce, health supplements and other things that appeal to healthy people.

Let's list the things that we think are critical, very important and so on.

Critical: Store front to sell out of. Local sources for organic produce, fair trade products, vitamin and health supplements distributor.

Very Important: Cheap rent and utilities. Affluent neighborhood with health nuts.

Important: Internet connection. Store fixtures already installed.

Not so important: Brewery, steak and sausage factories nearby.

A catering company?

Start by looking for venues nearby that specialize in weddings, parties, funerals and other events. You'll also need a place to make or buy the food, rent tables, chairs and a way to deliver them.

A wedding planner?

You may start by operating out of your house, but you'll need many of the same things the caterer needs including a caterer(s) nearby.

A travel agent?

Good luck! With so many travel sites on the Internet we would suggest you look for another business to get into. Or specialize in a very unique market such as sheiks offering camel tours in the Arabian desert.

An ethnic food market?

Try to make sure there is a farmers' market nearby where you can set up a stand as a test before you jump in and rent a store front. Is the right ethnic mix close by? Selling kosher food in a pretty much Christian neighborhood might not work too well.

A knife sharpening business?

Are there a lot of restaurants nearby? When Bob had his restaurant he had all of their knives sharpened once a month and was a stable source of business for the knife sharpener who had a mobile service and came to the restaurant.

A dog grooming service? Look for a store front near or next to a veterinarian. Better yet, share space in the veterinarians shop. How about a mobile grooming service? Buy a van, install counters, a holding pen, a wash area and decorate the van with cutesy dog and cat cartoon figures (and your phone number!) and your off and grooming!

Okay! Enough examples already!

As we go into other things you need to consider we'll often come back to location and things that will (or should) affect your location choice, so keep your list handy.

Once you have selected several possible locations for your business, you'll need to go visit them. Have your list in hand and explore, verify, take pictures, take notes and plan on several return visits at different times. Look at what other businesses in the neighborhood are doing. What's working and what's not? Ask them what sells and what doesn't.

Why should they tell you? Because when you bring new customers into the neighborhood everybody wins. Ask them about rents, utility costs, and property maintenance. Is there a stable customer base? Is there a seasonal increase? What kind of traffic do they see during the day? At night? On weekends? etc.

Location is likely the most important decision you'll make about your business!!!! It may very well be the deciding factor as to whether or not you're successful or become a part of the failure statics, which aren't pretty and not in your favor!

Ask questions! Ask more questions! Then ask even more questions! Take someone with you that thinks differently than you! Take someone with you who isn't involved in your business plans. If you're male take a female with you. They are not afraid to ask the questions you think will make you look stupid! If you're a female take a male with you, but don't let him ask questions! Do whatever you have to in order to assure yourself that this is the ideal location for your business or as close to it as you can get!

Colours

My God, they've really lost it! Give. Me. A. Break. Colours? Are we really going to talk about colours? You bet! (BTW, colours is kiwi for colors.)

The colours you choose for things like signs, menus, stationery or your building can say as much or more than the words you put on them. They can also un-say or override the message written on them.

Think about what each colour says to you. Bright reds, yellows and lime green walls in your "Family Style" restaurant may not exactly enhance that warm, friendly, inviting atmosphere you are looking for. However, red and yellow are good colours for a restaurant because these colours stimulate the salivary glands. Think of McDonalds and Chinese restaurants.

On the other hand, if you are opening a modern art framing studio, you might want to add some orange and azure blue in there.

Ask yourself:

- Is that sign you're planning for your brown store front a contrasting color?
- Does dark green really reflect the fun atmosphere of your disco bar?
- Is beige lettering on a white background really a good menu choice?

Think about the following for colors:

- Do they reflect the image and feeling you want?
- Are they contrasting enough to be seen and easily read?
- Are they pleasant, inviting, warm, friendly, peaceful?
- Are they bold, vibrant, shout at you, grab your attention?
- Can they be seen, read, command your attention?
- Do they give you warm fuzzies, chills, peace, or put you to sleep?
- Do they appeal to females, males, kids?

In each case, is that what you're looking for?

While we are close to the subject, the same things apply to the font and lettering sizes you choose. That size 6 Matura script on your menu may be really cool and different, but if people can't read it it's going to have a big impact on your sales. So too is your 20 foot tall orange block letter sign that screams "Funeral Home" on your 12-foot tall building!

Summary

There are so many things to consider of when setting the image you want for your business; the name, your location, signage and even colours, to mention just a few. Here again, you need to be sure and research whatever you choose to be sure you present the image you want.

Exercise

Write down some key words, phrases, colors and even locations that might be associated with your business. Does that inspire a name for your business?

Better yet, get a bottle of wine, some nibbles and have your friends over for a brainstorming session. It might be surprising what names come up after a few sips!

Notes

Chapter 5 – Marketing and Advertising

It's absolutely crucial to market and advertise your business so that you can sell your products and/or services, get the business name out there and to start creating a following.

What is Marketing?

Marketing is about getting your goods/services to the customer and generally involves:

- Product (identification, selection and development).
- Price
- Place (distribution channels)
- Promotion

What is Advertising?

Advertising is the promotion part of marketing and is about creating information to promote the sale of goods/services.

Who Should You Market to?

By now you'll have a very clear picture of who your target market is and who are your customers (hint: if you're not sure revisit Chapter 3).

Having your target market clearly identified will ensure you don't waste precious advertising money.

When Robyn was advertising her Northern Administrators' Summit, she made a list of all the administration sources she could use:

- admiNZ magazine (the magazine for the Association of Administrative Professionals in New Zealand).
- Emails through her business database.
- Distributing flyers at her training events.

It had been suggested that she try advertising in her city's newspaper, which she did, but results were disappointing. It was too wide of an audience. Only one registration was gained from the $600 it cost to place the ad.

With Bob's restaurant, advertising was very different. Why? Because they had several target markets they needed to reach. For lunch, their customers were primarily local business owners or people who worked in those businesses. For dinner and Sunday brunch, it was townspeople, tourists or people just passing through on the main highway.

So, like Robyn, they made a list of resources they could use.

- Ads on local radio stations.
- Ads in local newspapers.
- Distributing and posting flyers.
- Banners and signs in front of the restaurant.
- Coupons.
- Word of mouth.

In fact, they used all of these at various times. Which brings up another point: Don't be afraid to adjust your advertising based on response. In Robyn's case, the lack of results from her local newspaper ad showed it was simply not a good resource for her type of business.

For Bob's restaurant their ads on the local radio station and coupons had fantastic results, when they first opened. But once the word spread the radio ads and the coupons brought in fewer and fewer people and they finally quit using both of them.

Point of Difference

Also think about what your point of difference is and how you can capitalize on that. What makes you different from the competition? For Robyn it was her specialization in providing minute taking training. For Bob's restaurant it was their menu (the types of food they served) and outstanding service.

Common Marketing and Advertising Methods to Consider

- TV (local and/or national) but expensive.
- Radio (local and national) but remember your target audience. Are the majority of listeners of a rock radio station going to be interested in horse manure or hand lotion that makes skin softer? No, but the listeners of a Country Western station might.)
- Newspapers (local and area) but again, remember your target audience.
- Magazines.
- Movie theatres.
- Throwaways - local ad papers like the Pennysaver.
- Groupon, 2 for 1 coupon mailers or newspaper coupons.
- Flyers (distributed in the right area).
- Community/library noticeboards.
- Database/e-mails.
- Internet ranking and rating sites (See Chapter 7).

- Web page (See Chapter 8).
- Social media (See Chapter 9).
- Flashmob (See YouTube).
- Sandwich boards/sign twirlers.
- Banner behind a plane.
- Billboards.
- Bus/train advertising (on the back, on the side, inside).
- Back of public toilet doors.
- Business networks you might be a member of: Chamber of Commerce (CC), Better Business Bureau (BBB), Business Network International (BNI).

Word of Mouth

Don't underestimate the power of word of mouth. Talk to everyone about your business: what you're selling, where, and how. It's the best form of advertising and... it's free!

Talk to Other Businesses

All merchants win when more customers are attracted to the area. Want to open a plumbing or electrical supply store? Go to your local Home Depot or Lowes, find the Store Manager or Department Head of Plumbing or Electrical and introduce yourself. Tell them what you carry, where you are located, invite them over for a tour, hand out your business cards and ask them to refer people. When Bob worked at Home Depot they constantly referred people to local tradesmen or stores when they came in looking for something their store didn't carry or when they needed someone to do their plumbing or electrical work.

Also think about what your competitors are doing. Can you provide the same thing but at a cheaper price without compromising profit margins? Can you match their lowest price?

When Should I Market/Advertise?

Marketing and advertising is a 24/7, 365 day a year event.

Are your products or services tied to certain times of the year? Does it make sense to capitalize on opportunities to sell more or draw attention to your products and services on:

- Valentine's Day.
- Easter.
- Thanksgiving.
- Halloween.
- Christmas.
- Spring.
- Summer.
- Fall/Autumn.
- Winter.
- World Vegetarian Day.
- Winter Solstice.
- St Patrick's Day.
- Children's Day.
- 4th of July.
- Mother's Day.
- Father's Day.
- Your business's anniversary.

At these times you may want to think about providing discounts on certain products/services or to certain people, e.g. in autumn, 10 percent discount off winter pajamas. Or buy one get one free, buy one get another half-price, bring a friend and your meal is free. Special offers to customers who use your catering service for: Halloween, Christmas, parties.

Creating Loyalty

Loyalty reward cards are very popular in cafes, e.g. a customer gets a card and every time the customer buys a coffee the card is stamped and after their tenth purchase they receive a free coffee. Customers get a reward for their loyalty and hopefully they'll keep coming back.

Marketing Budget and Tracking Sales

Have a think about how much money you want to or can afford to set aside to promote your business. You can spend very little or you can spend thousands.

Regardless of how much you spend you need to be able to, as much as you can, track any marketing or marketing campaigns you do, otherwise you'll have no idea what's working.

Tracking sales against marketing spending can be difficult, but promotional codes work well, e.g. to receive a discount off a product the customer quotes a code that was provide in an advertisement. That way you will be able to track how many sales you made from a particular promotion.

Summary

In this chapter we've defined the difference between advertising and marketing and given you some ideas on how to market your business and ways to advertise.

Exercise

Using the following list, create a marketing and advertising plan.

- Confirm your target market.
- Confirm the geographic area you'll sell to.
- Identify your competitors.
- Identify your point of difference.
- What will be the price of your product/services?
- How will you promote your product/services?
- How much money will you set aside for your marketing budget?
- How will you measure it?

From there, list the various types of advertising and marketing media that you think will work best for your business and that you want to research further.

A marketing and advertising plan can be critical to the success of your business so, feel free to add other things to the plan as you go. Once again, it's our intent to stir your mind and your job to determine what will and will not work for you.

Notes

Chapter 6 - Ratings & Rankings

This was one of the first chapters we put into our outline and it turned out to be one of the hardest to write. It started out addressing ranking your business, but immediately self-expanded to include ratings. We toyed with just leaving out the original ranking part, but still think it's important so we'll try and clarify the difference between the two and the importance of each.

Life used to be so much simpler. If you stayed focused on the important stuff, meeting the needs of your customers and your business goals, the rest would take care of itself. If a customer left happy, they bragged you up. If they were unhappy about something, the manager or you (the owner) would try to make it right. If they were still unhappy they would bad mouth you to their local circle of friends, which typically had minimal effect. In today's world, however, things are different. Very Different.

Let's start by defining the difference between "Rankings" and "Ratings".

Rankings

Rankings are the position of your business within your local business segment or possibly the whole business world, e.g. you can be ranked the "Best Italian Restaurant in Los Angeles" by the LA Times or you can be ranked the "Most Successful New Small Business" in San Diego by the SD Small Business Association.

In today's digital world, rankings will also often come from people voting for their favorite businesses in various categories listed in newspapers, magazines, by TV stations, travel sites, or social media web sites such as Yelp.

Ratings

Ratings are how people (usually your customers) rate your ability to provide quality products or services. Obviously ratings can, and often do, play a major role in how your business is ranked. But not always! Often agencies or newspapers will rank you solely on their findings with little input from the public segment. Is this fair? Sure it is, as long as they indicate it is based solely on their opinion and their criteria is applied fairly.

Importance

Are rankings and ratings important? Yes. Let's take rankings first. Often, rankings only list the winners or top "Win, Place or Show" selections. So if you make the list it's a feather in your business cap. If you don't? It's pretty much a, "who cares"!

Are we telling you to ignore opportunities to be ranked? No. In many cases, with little to no downside, having your business listed provides an opportunity to get your name out there.

Our message for the above type of rankings is simple: Take advantage of them but don't get caught up in the rankings game. Just remember, if everybody were first, there would be no first; so being second, third or tenth is okay. No matter your ranking, it gets your name out there in a positive way.

Other than dealing with ratings which may have some influence on rankings, you'll likely have little to no control over your ranking (short of bribery which, as a small business owner, you probably can't afford anyway!).

Ratings, on the other hand, are specific, have a major impact on your business reputation, and you need to be concerned about them.

We don't care how friendly, good, patient, caring, compassionate, thoughtful or what a good "people person" you are, at some point you are going to piss someone off. And in business, it will likely be sooner rather than later!

Something you do or say, or don't do or say, may send a customer up through the rafters. There are also people who are just never happy no matter what you do and still others who are having a bad day and feel they have to spread the wealth by ruining everyone else's day.

Whatever the case may be, your very best attempts at trying to make the customer happy are going to fail and someone is going to go off on you like a bottle rocket. Worse yet, they're going to go home and scalp you on Yelp, Facebook or Twitter!

AKA, you've just been rated!

Is this important? You bet!
Do you need to care about it? You bet!
Will this affect your rating? You bet!
Will this affect your ranking? It might.

Some rating facts:

- People who rate you are much more likely to do so because they are unhappy about something.
- People who leave promising to give you a good rating tend to get busy and forget, unless they had an absolutely outstanding experience that they just have to let the world know about.

- The people who left unhappy, no matter how busy they are, are probably going to go straight home and seek revenge.
- Today's unhappy camper now has a much larger "circle of friends" to bad mouth you to.
- The net result? If you do nothing, the bad ratings will typically outweigh the good ratings and have a more far reaching effect.

The final message? In today's business world it has become critical that you be able to influence your ratings as much as possible, including appeasing the negative reviewers and defending your business if need be.

On the flip side of that, don't forget to thank those who give you a good rating! A simple thank you (although we recommend you say much more than just *thank you*) not only provides recognition of the good review, it will win you points with other reviewers and make them much more likely to leave a positive review.

Case Study: Managing Negative Comments

As any person who has been in business more than a week knows, people will go out of their way to bad mouth a business when they're unhappy with a product or service they received. And social media sites offer an ideal sounding board for them. Is this bad? No, but we've all heard horror stories about someone whose reputation was unfairly slashed to pieces on Facebook and some of the reviews we've read on Yelp have been nothing short of vicious and vindictive.

Friends of ours agreed to accept coupons from Groupon at their business. As with most coupons, there were conditions which, unfortunately most people don't read or simply ignore. In any case, a group of three couples came into their establishment, a wine bar, ordered a bunch of drinks and nibbles and didn't tell them about the coupons till they were ready to pay their bill and leave. Needless to say, most of what they had ordered was not included in the coupon deal they had negotiated with Groupon and it was clearly stated on the coupon that these items weren't included.

After several minutes of raised voices (by everyone) our friends decided it was not worth losing customers over and offered to split the difference and take half of the coupon's value off their bill. Reluctantly, the group agreed, paid their bill and left.

A week later our friends noticed their rating on Yelp had dropped from 4½ stars to 1½ stars. In reading the latest reviews (all posted within three days of the incident) they were astonished at how they could get so many bad reviews in three days! Yes folks, the wonderful group had gone home and all posted a one star review. Not only that, they had gotten several of their friends to also post reviews, all with almost identical complaints!

It took our friends many emails, tweets, phone calls and over six months to get their rating on Yelp back up, with very little help from Yelp, we might add. The moral of this story? Social media sites offer great exposure for your business, but they also offer an outlet for disgruntled customers that can have a major impact on your business! This is why we really think the suggestion to have a staff or team member responsible for social media and rating sites is a great idea. That person should also be required to check media sites on at least a daily basis so that if your business does get bashed, you can respond quickly. If you can't assign someone, there are web sites that will monitor bad reviews, notify you and work to have them removed or cleared.

A word of caution. Several of these monitor sites have not so good reputations. So like any other thing you do to promote or protect your business, be sure to thoroughly check them out before you hire them.

To be fair, we have to add that many rating sites do monitor and screen the ratings they receive; Trip Advisor, Amazon, Cruise Critic, and now Yelp, being just some of them. Many rating web sites also design their rating system so that the rater may "down rate" a business, but the rating will be rejected if they try to "berate" them.

We'll talk more about ratings and ways to defend yourself in Chapter 8 - Social Media. We also strongly suggest you tie them into your Marketing and Advertising Plan.

Summary

We've tried to define the difference between rankings and ratings, although they're closely tied and often run together. We've also pointed out their importance in both helping and hurting your business and the need to respond to both.

Exercise

Think about where your rankings and ratings are likely to come from. Try and make a list of rankings you might want to try to gain or influence and the ratings you want to closely monitor. Also, in conjunction with Chapter 8, list who will be responsible to monitor and respond to both.

Notes

Chapter 7 - Your Website

In today's business world you absolutely **must have a website**. This is to ensure your business has a 24/7 global presence where people can go to obtain information about your business (location, hours, directions, etc.) as well as check out your products and services.

In this age of increasing on-line buying, and if it's appropriate for your type of business, which it will be to most, you must be able to provide a way for people to purchase your products and services no matter where they live.

What Should a Website do?

A website should be written to appeal to your target market and:

- Establish credibility.
- Support your business's brand.
- Provide useful and valuable information.
- Engage the customer or reader.
- Promote enthusiasm for your products or services.
- Persuade the customer to buy or act.
- Call the customer to action.

Things You Should do as Soon as You Can

Domain Name

Select a domain name (typically your business name), verify it's available and purchase it.

This is important because if it's already taken it'll likely mean you'll need to find a new name and you'll want to do that as soon as possible and with as little impact as possible.

Information Needed

Make a list of information you need to include:

- Your business address, phone number and email address.
- Days and hours of operation.
- A list of products or services you provide.
- If you serve food and/or drinks, your menu(s) and/or drinks list(s).
- Related facilities or services (meeting rooms, catering, special packages).
- If applicable, a brief description of ADA (Americans with Disabilities Act) compliance, handicap facilities or concerns like, handicap parking, availability of ramps/elevators, number of stairs, uneven surfaces, braille menus, etc.

Additional Information

There are a lot of other things you can add that might be helpful such as:

- A map of the area showing where you're located.
- Parking information.
- Holiday closures.
- Photos of your location (inside and outside).
- Virtual tours.
- Photos of your products, with links to additional details, specifications and prices.
- Product reviews.

- Advertisements, specials.
- Blogs.
- Links to your social media sites.
- Photos of staff.
- Videos of product demos, how to instructions, etc.
- Shopping cart.
- FAQ with answers.
- Testimonials, references.
- Newsletter (and a way to collect addresses so you can email a newsletter to your customers).

Designing Your Own Website

There are several sites that will let you build your own website for free or for a nominal fee. WordPress, Weebly and Wix are just three of them. These sites are pretty much one-stop shopping and will let you purchase your domain name, provide a raft of pre-designed sites to choose from and help you develop and customize the design you choose. Both Robyn and Bob have websites constructed through WordPress and have found WordPress to be fairly easy to use.

Once you think you've listed most of the information you'll need to post, pick a design that fits your needs: one that prominently and attractively displays the important information on the home page, allows you to add pages for additional information and lets you organize and group things in a way that makes sense. Also research websites for ones that you like and that are easy to read and use. Then, what do your competitors' websites look like?

When you finish designing your website ask yourself:

- If I were visiting this site for the first time, is everything I might need to know available?

- If something is not covered can I easily and quickly locate how to call or email you, and which would you prefer?
- Finally, put yourself in the shoes of someone who's not from the area or has physical limitations. Are you ADA compliant? Have you answered any questions they might have, like how do I get there? Are there wheelchair ramps or elevators available? If I have hearing or sight limitations is anything provided or is there someone available to help me?

Part of being a GREAT business owner is thinking about and providing the best customer service you can to ALL of your customers!

Using Website Designers

If you aren't comfortable designing and building your own website there are a plethora of companies that will help you or do it for you. At a price, of course. Whether you pick someone local (which we would recommend) or on the Internet, be sure you check references before you retain them.

Ask to see examples of their work and make sure it's appealing and contains information similar to what you expect to see on your website. Contact the sites they say they built and find out if they finished on time, how much they paid, how many revisions were needed and if they're happy with the results.

We hope by now we don't need to remind you that it's **YOU** popping up every time someone pulls up your website, and you need to make the best impression possible!

NB: Writing content for a website requires specialized skills. It is highly recommended that if you're designing and writing your website content that you take a course on

Writing for the Web. Courses cover such things as writing good content, formatting for effective scanning, and how to use keywords to ensure maximum Search Engine Optimization (SEO).

Website Cost

The cost to build a web site will vary based on several factors: who you use to design your website, which plan you pick, the template you choose or if you decide to go with an independent website designer. So here again, shop around and yip, research, research, research.

Summary

Having a website is critical in today's business world to ensure you have a 24/7 global presence.

It provides valuable information about your business and can help attract potential customers.

Your website should be attractive, easy to read and navigate. It should provide as much information about your business as possible and answer, at the very least, the most common questions a customer would have.

Exercise

Create a checklist for you to get your website underway:

- Look over the available web site providers and decide which one you might want to use. Be sure to pay attention to the ease of building a website from their templates and the extent of online and real person help they offer.

- If you haven't already, decide on your domain name (and at least one alternative), verify that it's available and purchase it.
- Make a list of all the information that you want to put on your website then review the list to make sure everything a customer would want to know is on it.
- Create a list of major headings for your home page and make sure everything on the list above has a home.
- Decide whether you're going to design your own website or use a website designer. If you're going to use a designer, be sure to obtain a list of sites they've designed and check them out.

Notes

Chapter 8 - Social Media

Your Friend or Your Worse Enemy

There are a ton of social media sites out there and even more opinions about them. Especially if you're a business owner. Worse yet, we swear every morning, another one is created that you apparently can't live without.

In the social media world, you'll quickly find a rat's nest of opinions, promises, supposed opportunities, creative advertising, gimmicks, ways to reach the far corners of the earth, sites that swear everyone visits several times daily, sites your business can't survive without, and on and on.

For anyone, deciding which sites to be a part of and which ones to ignore can be a monumental task. Then, once you've created an account for each, keeping up with them and keeping your pages current can easily consume every waking moment.

As a business owner, you'll need to wade through this rat's nest to decide:

- Which sites have a payback, specifically for your business?
- Which sites should you have a presence on?
- Which sites are your potential customers likely to visit?

If social media is a new topic for you then don't be afraid to get some training or attend a social media conference.

What is Social Media?

Social media is made up of on-line sites that can help you connect with current and potential customers, no matter where they are and what time of day it is.

In Social Media Examiner's 2017 Social Media Marketing Industry Report, 88 percent of all marketers said their social media efforts generated more exposure for their business. Note that they said, "generated more exposure," not necessarily more business!

It is really important to understand that for businesses, social media is about building relationships and a following. And, while most sites offer advertising, we believe it should complement your marketing and advertising techniques and never replace traditional advertising, marketing and face-to-face communication.

Perhaps the easiest way to explain social media is to remind you of its name: "Social Media". The most accurate definition of social, as it pertains to social media is: "Living and breeding in more or less organized communities especially for the purposes of cooperation and mutual benefit."

Therefore it's important to think of each social media site as a community of people with some type of common interest that ties them together. That interest though, centers much more around companionship and interfacing with others than it does shopping for products or services.

So as a business owner, we believe, the primary purpose of maintaining a presence on social media should be to form and maintain a relationship and engage with your customers in a fun and informative way: Marketing or advertising your products should be secondary.

Hazards of Social Media

Social media has some very good benefits but, because of its very nature, it also has some hazards that you'll need to be aware of.

First, most social media users follow their favorite sites on a daily basis, some hourly. So if they post a question or comment, they expect an answer or response quickly. In their mind, there is someone just like them on the other end (that would be your site or page) just waiting to respond.

The expected response can vary, depending on the site (Facebook typically within a day; Twitter immediately). If you can't keep up with the expectations, you're best to stay off that site because you'll get bad mouthed for not responding in the expected timeframe.

Therefore if you want to maintain a presence on these sites, we strongly suggest you assign someone to deal with issues on a daily (or in the case of Twitter, hourly) basis. Which, you may want to do anyway for the next reason.

The second hazard of social media is the forum it provides for people to vent their anger and frustrations. As mentioned in the section covering reviews, people with a gripe are at least ten times more likely to post a complaint then happy people are to post how wonderful your product or service was.

Here again, the nature of social media makes time of the essence. Thankfully most social media and review sites now allow a response, especially from a business, to a critical review. But for every hour that goes by, hundreds of people may read that bashing you took on Facebook, Twitter or one of the review sites.

Finally, in today's world there are a raft of imposters, hackers and people who just want to destroy anything and everything they can with false posts. And, while social media sites do as much as they can to catch and eliminate these posts, it is still your responsibility to monitor for them and have them taken down and limit the harm to your business reputation.

So here again we think it's critical that you have someone monitoring each review site and social media site you're on and responding to posts, good or bad.

As you may have noticed, we added review sites in with that task. It only makes sense to have one (or more) people monitoring both types of sites. What also makes sense is having them personally involved in your advertising and marketing. In this way they can make sure you're addressing any issues in your ads, i.e. complaints about limited menu selections are addressed with your "new and expanded menu!"

Finally, we'll remind you that the more sites you're on, the more monitoring you'll need to do.

Benefits of Using Social Media

There are 2.5 billion social media users worldwide so your existing and potential customers are most likely on social media, somewhere. More than 50 percent of small business owners in the US rely on social media as their primary digital-marketing technique because of its effectiveness for finding and connecting with new customers. Source: www.blog.hootsuite.com.

The main things social media sites can do for your business:

1   Emphasize your point of difference

     Use social media to tell people what makes your
     business different from others. Why your products

are better, your service faster, more efficient and professional.

2   Increase exposure

This allows you to have ongoing discussions with your customers who can share information with their contacts, e.g. posting your cupcake recipe on Facebook so it can be shared with customers or followers giving you much more reach.

3   Be recognized as a knowledge resource

By posting regularly on what's happening within your business and industry cements your reputation as a knowledge resource. Post articles that help your customer, but avoid doing a hard sell which may annoy people.

As a general rule, your content across all social media sites should be no more than 20 percent promotional. The remaining 80 percent should be content that is engaging and relevant to your audience.

4   Follow others' expertise and knowledge

Following your competitors on their sites keeps you up-to-date with what they're doing, saying and thinking.

5   Provide research

Most social media sites have functions in which you can run surveys or polls. This is a great way to get instant feedback from your customers on certain things, e.g. what is their favorite cupcake flavors? Vanilla? Chocolate? Banana? This helps you, and keeps your customers engaged and interested in your products/services.

6   Reputation management

Social media allows business owners to respond to complaints and compliments quickly (yip, more on this later).

7   Low cost

Initial setup of social media is free and is therefore a low cost but effective advertising and marketing tool. Keep in mind many sites charge if you use their marketing/advertising services to reach a broader range of visitors to their site.

8   Staying in front of your customers

By regularly posting on social media you'll maintain a presence in front of your customers, even if they have only bought from you once or not bought from you – yet!

Social Media Sites

There are many, and it's important to choose the right one for your business and audience.

Below is a list of the most common social media sites that can be used.

Facebook

Facebook, the largest social network (2 billion users as at September 2017), is a great way to help your business grow through referrals and word-of-mouth.

The benefits of having a Facebook business page are:

- Increases exposure to potential customers.
- Helps you gather more leads.
- Low cost to set up and maintain.

- Targets a particular audience.
- Gathers statistics – how many followers, "likes", engagements.
- Builds brand loyalty.
- Directs people to your website.

For more information on how to set up a Facebook business page go to www.facebook.com/business/learn/set-up-facebook-page.

Instagram

Instagram (800 million members) is a photographic and highly visual way to share product and service content to your followers. Imagine the appeal of having photos of your pretty chocolate, vanilla or blueberry cupcakes displayed on your account or your designer jewelry or hats or pictures of your rescued horses you're raising funds to help.

In addition to the above benefits detailed for Facebook, Instagram can also be used to attract top talent and identify and establish relationships with influencers.

For more information on how to use Instagram see www.blog.hootsuite.com/how-to-use-instagram-for-business.

Twitter

Twitter allows you to microblog messages or tweets of up to 280-characters long. It is a great tool to get your message out to your customers and get instant feedback in real time. Twitter allows you to find, follow and share influencers and share things topical for your target audience.

One beneficial function of Twitter is that it enables others to retweet your messages. Hashtags help people to find your tweets and help you participate in conversations and follow influencers who can promote your business. Any tweet can provide a link back to web content and we suggest you always tweet a photo – keep it visual!

Twitter is fast moving and to keep you visible amongst your followers you need to tweet regularly – very regularly. As much as six times a day. This, therefore, can make Twitter a very time-consuming beast.

Twitter can take a little longer to understand and get your head around, but once you start tweeting and get into a rhythm it will all make sense.

LinkedIn

LinkedIn is a professional version of Facebook and is like having your curriculum vitae (resume) in an electronic format on a global database. You can connect with similar people in your profession, people who graduated from the same schools you did, post articles, join groups and have conversations. It's a great way to have a presence, build your brand and get your name out there. 467 million people are registered on LinkedIn.

Snapchat

One of the fastest growing networks especially for those in the 25 and under age bracket.

Snapchat is a great way to share filters, stories and videos, e.g. you could post a behind the scenes video of how to plant an herb garden. Snapchat's main difference to other platforms is that content is only available for a short time.

YouTube

The best way to connect with your customers is by using video. On YouTube you can create your own channel, where you can upload a two or three minute video that promotes your business and how-to-videos. You can also use videos to provide testimonials from customers, showcase your products/services and demonstrate your expertise.

Pinterest

Pinterest is an online pinboard. It's a tool, similar to Instagram, which allows you to create boards and pin images (photos and graphics). Users interact with each other by liking, commenting and re-pinning pins.

Pinterest is where people look for ideas and inspiration, e.g. search for wedding venues in Blenheim and a number of pins pop up showing gorgeous places to hold a wedding.

People who are re-pinning your pins are helping to increase awareness, drive more traffic to your website and create new leads.

Choosing the Right Social Media Sites for Your Business

Don't try and be on all social media sites – it will become overwhelming very quickly and also soak up a lot of time. We suggest you monitor each social media site for a while before you decide to use it. See who's on it, what type of content does everyone have, what conversations are going on, etc.?

Think about which social media sites will work best for your business. Robyn wearing her writing hat, is on Facebook, Twitter and Pinterest while Bob uses Facebook and pretty much ignores his Twitter account.

Choose which ones will best promote your business, get you the most feedback and allow you to maximize customer engagement.

It is also critical for you to ensure you know who is your online audience: define them by age, gender, interests, profession, and location, as much as you can.

Finally, you need to post different content on each of your sites, which means you'll need a different promotional strategy for each to fit with its target audience.

The Cost of Being on Social Media Sites

Many of the social media sites are free. However, some sites have different rules for businesses and may require you to have a "business site" that they charge a fee for. On most sites there is no charge for establishing a site but, there will be a charge if you utilize their advertising. Here again the charges vary from site to site so, be sure to research their various advertising plans. Know what you get and most importantly, make sure they provide a set of metrics so you know how many people visit your site, what they look at and any other parameters that are important to you.

Survey Sites

While survey sites are not social media sites, they can be a valuable tool to find out what people think of your business, which of your social media sites people are visiting and the answers to any other questions you might want.

There are several survey sites, with the most popular probably being Survey Monkey. On each of these sites, you can use one of their canned questionnaires or design your own survey from their list of questions and/or by creating your own.

Once again, the cost of using these sites will vary, depending on the number of questions, how many people are surveyed and how often the survey is run. Therefore, research carefully to make sure you get the survey and results you want.

Summary

Social media sites can be cost effective tools that can help your business attract and engage with customers.

It is important to choose social media sites that your target audience hangs out on.

For business owners, the primary purpose of maintaining a presence on social media should be to form and maintain a relationship and engage with your customers in a fun and informative way: Marketing or advertising your products should be secondary.

Most social media users who post on a site expect a response, usually within a day or sooner. Therefore, you'll want to assign one or more people to deal with issues or complaints on a daily basis, as a minimum.

Exercise 1

Assign someone with a sound social media knowledge to be responsible for keeping up with social media and daily review posts. (This will be you if you don't have staff yet.)

Work through the following steps with them:

1. Identify up to three social media sites that you think are the best fit for your business and your audiences.
2. List your target audience from Chapter 2 by age, sex, location and appeal to your products and services. Verify that the social

media sites you've selected appeal to and are visited by your target audiences.

3. Compile a social media plan, including what and how often you'll post, as defined below.
4. Create accounts for each site.
5. Start Facebooking, Snapchatting, Tweeting and pinning!

Exercise 2 - Your Social Media Plan

- Set some goals and objectives. A goal might be that the business will be active on three social media sites by (date). An objective might be to find sites that appeal to all of your target audiences.

- Use the SMART (specific, measurable, attainable, realistic, timeframe) formula to set goals and objectives for each target audience type.

- For your target audiences:

    - List their problems or concerns.
    - List three marketing messages for this audience.
    - List the preferred social media networks for each of your audiences.

- Work out what content would help your audience and increase engagement.

Some suggestions to help attract their interest:

- Welcome new followers.
- Share a photo.
- Ask questions.
- Fill in the blanks, e.g. The best way to use our product X is _____.

- One little-known way to solve this problem is: (solution).
- "Caption this photo/video".
- "If" (enticing scenario) I would _____.
- "Like" if you (do an activity).
- Remember when? (old fashioned tradition).
- Share an article from your website.
- Word of the day.
- React to a competitor's post – agree or offer an alternative opinion.

Use visuals as much as you can – images, GIFs, memes, videos.

- Print out a monthly calendar and schedule your content on each site for each day of the month. (This will be a good way to assess and adjust your time commitment to social media.)

- Schedule time (around 15-30 minutes a day) for someone to manage your social media accounts, e.g. respond to comments, "likes", and replies. This could be as simple as posting a website link on Facebook, tweeting three times a day or repinning (Pinterest) five images a day.

- Social media management is time consuming. Using social media management tools such as Hootsuite will help you to automate and post content automatically across your social media sites on a single dashboard with one click. Hootsuite also enables you to respond quickly to messages, mentions and comments.

- Manage feedback. Eighty percent of customers expect a reply within 24 hours of a posting. Respond to comments and feedback, both positive and negative. If it's a negative comment, respond immediately, or make sure the staff member responsible for managing social media responds as soon as possible.

- Investigate the benefits of paid social advertising. Facebook offers a number of advertising options and Twitter uses promoted content and promoted accounts.

- Use the social media sites analytical data to measure and evaluate your results to determine number of clicks per post, number of page visits, the reach of your campaigns, growth, engagement and sharing. This will enable you to review your results regularly and work out what strategies are working and adjust accordingly.

***

Two final thoughts:

Don't forget about travel web sites like Trip Advisor. Most of these websites rate businesses in various cities. Bob belongs to TripAdvisor and has rated many of his favorite restaurants and venues here in San Diego and other places he's visited.

Have your friends Twitterdee and Twitterdum and family's Facebook BFFs join these web sites and rate you. The more exposure you get the better! Is this cheating? We don't think so, but if they (or you) are not comfortable, don't do it.

***

We'll close this chapter by repeating what we've said throughout in several different ways: There are as many opinions about the use, value and effectiveness of social media sites as there are people. Probably more since there are so many sites and new ones coming on-line every day.

Some people love them, some hate them, some are totally confused by them and most are somewhere in between.

It would be fair for us to say we think of them as a necessary evil. Necessary because so many people use them daily, and for a business they offer great exposure. Evil because they are very time consuming, can be confusing, and their actual value and effectiveness on your sales is hard, if not impossible, to judge.

If you use them, how you use them and how much time you devote to them is up to you. We strongly suggest, however, that when you set up your sites, you include a way to measure their effectiveness on sale.

Robyn has an excellent way to accomplish this by simply including a unique code on each site that a person enters if they order something from you. This allows you to determine the effectiveness of each site and adjust your use of it accordingly.

Okay. We're done! (Well, with this chapter.)

Happy Tweeting, Facebooking, Snapchatting, pinning and board posting!

Notes

Chapter 9 - Accounting and Records

In upcoming chapters we're going to cover various expenses related to your business. Before we get into expenses though, let's talk about accounting and some of the records you might need for your business.

Why do we want to cover accounting first? Simple; because we want you to look at and pick out a potential accounting and record keeping system before we get into some of the many expenses you're going to need to keep track of.

By now we hope you understand how our minds work so, we're going to wander off for a paragraph or two and jump to something you may have noticed.

We keep saying, "Why?" and hope that you'll pick up our habit and start saying it.

Why? It's simple! Go back to your childhood (we never left ours according to our mates and friends) when you questioned **everything**! Remember that? That's how you learned! That's what you need to do again, until you've learned everything you can about the business you want to start.

Which will be just after you turn a profit and a vampire attacks you in a dark alley, drains you of blood and takes the bank bag with all your profits. (Robyn here. Sorry. Bob snuck that in. We really need to finish this and let him get to his vampire novel. In the meantime, we'll refrain from any more blood sucking comments till the section on loans.)

Your accounting system is going to be crucial to operating your business. It is (or should be) the most valuable tool in your business tool box. If set up and maintained properly it will tell you where your business stands at any given moment in time.

It will give you reports that can help you track and project sales, expenses and profit. It will provide the data you need to secure loans, manage your assets and liabilities and generally control the day-to-day operation of your business.

So selecting the right system is very important.

Most software systems will easily handle just about any small business. Some of the more popular are QuickBooks, Peachtree/Sage, Quicken and Microsoft Office Small Business Accounting. Each contains the basic features required by any small business and most can be integrated with other systems such as inventory, POS (Point of Sale), on-line banking and payroll.

Start by checking the Internet for reviews on various systems. The things you want to look for are:

- Is it easy to learn, set up and use?

- Does it have easy to reach, "real person" support? (The last thing you want is to have to spend an hour punching in menu selections trying to get to a real person!)

- Will it integrate with other systems you have (or plan to have) such as POS, payroll, inventory and on-line banking? Make sure it will integrate with the **specific** systems you're going to use. If you have not chosen the other systems yet, find out which systems the accounting software supports. This will help narrow your search for these systems later.

- Will it generate the forms you need such as quotes, estimates, invoices, inventory, purchase orders (POs), timesheets, sales orders (SOs), etc?

- Will it generate the reports you need such as inventory management, sales and sales projection, cash flow analysis and projection, SO and PO management?

Side note: If you are opening a new business and plan on applying for a loan, try and find a system that will generate some, if not all, of the "projected" financial reports you will need when applying for the loan (See Chapter 13 on Financing).

Once you have selected a software system, price it on sites like Amazon and Office Depot and **read the reviews**! Often the reviews you find on the Internet are written by professional evaluators or people much higher up on the learning curve than a new business owner. The reviews on Amazon and Office Depot are usually written by common users like us and are typically much easier to understand and more likely to rate the features we are most interested in.

Once you purchase your software, load it onto your computer and start using it. The more familiar you are with it before you open your business, the better. You can also use it to help generate those projected reports needed for a loan and to help you do a sanity check on the numbers you've had rolling around in your head on operating expenses and sales projections.

Finally, as you define and locate your equipment and facilities, load each one in so you get a firm handle on your startup expenses.

For those of you who are now firmly convinced you have nowhere near the smarts to do this, relax and take a deep breath. There are many business owners, big and small, who would not touch their books with a ten foot pole. If you feel totally overwhelmed by this, there are several options.

If you just feel plain stupid and totally out of your realm of reality but think you might eventually master this, you can purchase books to help you come up to speed on accounting. Two such books are *Book Keeping and Accounting for Small Business* (7th edition, by Peter Taylor) and *Bookkeeping Boot Camp* (Get a Grip on Accounting Basics - 101 for Small Business, by Angie Mohr). These, and many others like them, will cover the basics of business accounting and give you warm fuzzies whenever you get near your computer. (Especially if it's been on for a while.)

If you just can't figure out how to pick a system, you can retain a CPA to help you select a system. Or if you know and trust someone who is already in business or really savvy with software, perhaps they can help you. Whichever you choose, **make sure the system they pick meets your needs** and is not just their favorite or the one they use. Also, make sure they help you get comfortable with using it and are "on call" for additional help as part of the deal.

If you're uncomfortable keeping your own books, contract with someone to do them for you. This can be a CPA that comes into your business or someone off site with **secure** on-line access to your accounting system.

If you do contract with someone to do your bookkeeping for you, make sure they know what they are doing and are trustworthy.

(if you're thinking of letting a friend or family member keep your books, generally, your mistress or your mother is not a good choice for this position. We're just saying!)

Remember, this is the most important tool you have for running your business! It is also the best tool to run your business into the ground if it's not used properly!

In addition to the accounting software almost every business is going to have "paper" (Yes, we said paper. You remember; sheets of that thin white stuff) needed somewhere in the system. This could be meal tickets in your restaurant, POs sent in by your customers, employee's auto expense logs or credit card slips. Whatever they are, you need to make sure you're set up to process and account for them.

In today's world this often will be scanning them into the system or eliminating them totally by using POS tablets or other devices.

Your accounting system will never be any better than the data that is input. So if you don't control the input, the system will be no better than the software it's written on! (Cute, Huh?)

We know, many of these areas have been or are being replaced with electronic media (tablet POS systems, smart phone swipers, email orders, etc.). Yet they, the paper customer interface, and even the new electronic media replacing them, remain the weak link in many business systems. So pay attention to them. Make sure they get input, and input right, every time. Also, make sure they are retained and can be checked when things don't balance or all of a sudden changes that don't make sense are noted.

***

No matter what your type of business, there will be purchased goods and services associated with it. This may range from office supplies to a full range of food items (if you own a restaurant or bar) to production materials for a manufacturing operation.

Services might include deliveries, both incoming and outgoing, accounting, tax preparation and on and on. And then there's janitorial services, bathroom supplies and parts related to maintenance and repairs.

Some other things you'll want your system to do or calculate might include:

- Determine the cost of goods and services: Your cost for an item you use or resell isn't just the price you pay for the item. There's shipping, processing it in and out, stocking and your shipping costs to get it to your customer. All of that needs to be added to the price for the item to determine how much you should charge.
Likewise if you provide a service at the customers site there's travel time, gasoline and vehicle maintenance.
- Food costs and drink costs for restaurants and bars: Here again, all of the things that go into a meal or drink need to be accounted for in determining what it really costs you to build that meal or drink.
- Profit margin: Once you know what you true cost is, and decided how much profit to add, you'll want your system to track your profit margin. This is especially important as the cost of the item, shipping and other related charges change over time and being aware of each change and calculating its effect on your profits is a full time job. One best left to a computer that can alert you that you're now selling stuff at less than your cost.
- Inventory: Don't forget to tie your accounting system to your inventory system

Summary

We've covered as many of the accounting and records components as we could think of. We've also given you some idea of the numerous systems, both self-maintained or tied to a professional service, that you might use.

You'll also find the next two chapters (Chapter 10 Equipment and Chapter 11 Property and Expenses) tie directly into these and other systems so be sure to include everything in these chapters in your system selection criteria.

Exercise

Research the various accounting and record systems and options that might work best for your business.

Decide if you want to maintain your own records or have someone else do it for you.

Either way, put your system in place as soon as possible so you can enter and track many of the start- up expenses you'll encounter.

Notes

Chapter 10 - Equipment

Wow! Where do we start? Equipment can easily be one of the biggest expenses in starting your own business. That means it will likely have a major impact on your balance sheet for the first several years of your business, if not longer.

No matter what business you're thinking of, the ideal situation would be to purchase or rent your property with most or all of the equipment already installed. Why? Let's compare prices for several different types of businesses.

Let's start with one home based business (construction) and one non-home based business (restaurant). Let's say our restaurant is about medium size. If the weather is nice, we can seat just over 250 people: 175+ inside and 75 on the patio.

Installed Equipment

If we equip the kitchen with all new equipment it could easily run over $150,000.

If we purchase used equipment from a supplier, the standard going rate would be half price or slightly higher. So equipping our restaurant with used equipment would run around $75,000.

If we purchase used equipment already installed in a business or from a private party, pricing can run anywhere from 10 to 40 cents on the dollar, depending on the condition of the equipment and how desperate the owner is to get rid of it.

By the way, the pricing above is pretty much standard for equipment that is fixed or installed (non-portable), regardless of what type of equipment it is. That is: 50 percent for used equipment from a supplier and 10 – 40 percent for used equipment that is still installed or purchased from a private source.

Why is that? Because if you purchase new or used equipment from a supplier they are going to provide a warranty or guarantee that the equipment is in good working order and that all the parts and accessories are there. If you purchase it used and installed it in place or from a private party it's pretty much "what you see is what you get" or "as is, buyer beware".

Aside from the cost of the equipment, let's talk about some of the other factors involved. If you buy new or used equipment from a supplier or private source you have to add delivery and installation. Be aware, you're not buying a 30" four- burner stove and a 24" dishwasher folks. Nor is this Home Depot where you get free delivery and set up!

The typical commercial stove is at least twice as big as and about 10 times heavier than your typical home stove. And the dish washer? Well, counting the in and out staging counters and racking, figure 10 – 12 feet long, 4 - 6 foot high and about 1,000 pounds.

So on top of the purchase price, plan on paying for delivery, unpacking and set up. That assumes the utilities needed like gas, electric and water are already there, and in the right places.

If you purchase equipment already installed you might actually have the opposite problem. Typically the price will be based on a package deal for all of the installed equipment. This means you may have to figure what you are going to do with the stuff you don't need or is in too poor condition to use, repair or sell.

This also assumes the equipment is installed in the place you'll be using for your business. If not, plan on fees for having it disconnected, transported and reconnected in your location.

We know! Life is getting soooo complicated! You never figured on any of this and right now you feel like someone crapped in your mess kit. But, alas, have no fear buckaroo, we've only just begun. See now why you might want to throw away that equipment catalog and replace it with this year's Celebrity Cruises catalog?

Okay, so we'll try and brighten your day a little. The good news is you have choices in all of this. Aside from buying new or used, in many cases you can also lease, rent or rent with an option to buy.

Obviously, these options are going to be more expensive, but they can really help if you want to delay purchasing something, are not sure how long you will need something or are not sure you're going to stay in business.

Yes, it really is okay to take a "trial run" at your dream business to make sure it truly is what you want to do for the rest of your life. If this is the case, we have two comments. First, that is basically what Bob and his wife did with their restaurant and second, try working for someone else in the same business to see if you like it. It's a lot cheaper.

Let's move on to some other business examples.

If you're going into the construction business you can easily "tool and equipment yourself to death". But the nice thing is there are numerous ways to limit the tools and equipment you'll need.

If you specialize in a particular trade (plumbing, electrical, framing, finish carpentry, etc.) it's going to drastically narrow down the tools and equipment you'll need. If you are into general contracting or renovation, specializing in new builds, residential, commercial or other categories will also help narrow the list. You can also sub-contract work out to specialty contractors, like electricians and plumbers, to avoid needing to purchase tools related to those trades.

Another nice thing about the construction industry is that there are a ton of places where you can rent just about any piece of equipment or tool you might need. While it is usually more expensive to rent than own, normally you can pass the rental fees directly on to your customer.

When it comes to buying tools and equipment you can use the following rules: For hand and small power tools, if you don't think you'll use it on more than half your jobs, don't buy it.

For equipment, as well as large or specialized power tools, rent it. We suggest this for several reasons. First, if you store all of your tools and equipment in a dedicated area, like a separate bay of the garage, which also acts as a workshop, the storage space will be limited.

Second, typically your jobs are going to be spread over a fairly large area and so your tools will need to be reasonably portable. Even though you limit what you buy, you can easily have over $30,000 invested in tools and equipment. That, by the way, does not include your truck or office equipment.

Speaking of office equipment. Almost any business is going to need a computer, printer, copier, fax machine, phone, desk, chair and other assorted office furniture.

Once again, there are ways to reduce the list, like buying an all-in-one printer that scans, prints, copies, faxes and dispenses toilet paper in the restroom. (Only kidding about the toilet paper.)

You can also use an iPad or tablet computer to give you portability if you need it BUT, along with that comes a warning. If you should lose or damage it, all of your business records go with it. Telling the IRS that you lost your iPad is like saying the dog ate your homework, which frankly they couldn't care less about.

So we strongly suggest that you keep your business records on a desktop, safely sitting under your office desk and backed up on a daily basis at a minimum! If you want to download a duplicate to your iPad or tablet to drag around with you, fine. When you're done at the end of each day, upload the latest changes to the desktop and then back it up again. Better yet, upload everything every time you return to your office.

With the giveaway prices of desktop computers today, using a home based desktop computer is a cheap and easy way to make sure your business records stay safe and sound!

A second way to accomplish the same thing is via a "Cloud" or Internet backup service. This can be used with both your desktop and tablets and may actually prove to be more convenient because they often update the cloud or backup account in real time or at selected intervals. In this way your backup account is always up to date and you do not have to bother remembering to do a backup update at the end of a long and tiring day.

Specialized Equipment

Many businesses require unique or very specialized equipment. For example, if you're going to open a wine tasting room you'll need industrial size wine racks, a big counter or bar, maybe a few wine vats if you're going to bottle your own label, a wine press or two and a lot of glasses! (Bob knows as much about wine tasting rooms as he does about organic food so Robyn, the Marlborough, New Zealand wine connoisseur will deal with any winery examples.)

117

Even though he knows as much about horses as he does wine, we'll give Bob the horsey examples since our horsey friend is really going to need some unique stuff including; corral fencing, water and feed troughs, sheds and barns, probably a tractor and a golf cart or two with little wagons to pull stuff around in.

When Bob and his wife bought the restaurant they purchased the land, buildings, all of the equipment, fixtures, appliances, supplies and yes, the recipes! In short, the whole kit and caboodle! Depending on whose pricing you wanted to believe, they paid between 25 percent and 30 percent of the equipment's cost if it were new. Most of the items were two-three years old and everything was in good working order. Plus there was no delivery or setup to worry about!

If our horsey friend purchases a working (or previously working) horse ranch, chances are pretty good that most of what she needs is already going to be there. Chances are also very good that, even if the previous owner is moving to a new ranch, they are not going to want to lug most of that stuff with them and she can probably negotiate a pretty good deal on everything.

For our wine tasting room friend we have two questions. Do you have any idea how BIG wine vats are? Also, do you know how many people go into the wine business and fail?

Then there are other issues. First, before you can move a wine vat you have to drink all the wine in it, which probably adds to why so many wine businesses fail. Second, because so many fail, there is a very good chance you can find one to buy that's already equipped, with wine and all.

Summary

No matter what your business is or what equipment you'll need, the rules remain the same.

1. Try and find a place that is already set up with everything you need. Even if you pay more up front, this will be your cheapest option in the long run. It will also give you the most bargaining power since the person selling gets rid of everything in one transaction, with little fuss or muss. (Be sure to use that tidbit of information when negotiating with them!)

2. Buying new equipment will always be the most expensive option. In addition, you are likely to have to fork out for at least delivery and setup. It also gives you the least bargaining power because, unless you're spending a major fortune, you're not going to have much leverage. (By major fortune I mean like "really major"! Our $150,000 kitchen would be peanuts compared to large chains that drop several million when equipping their restaurants. By the way, this will not be the only time you will be at the bottom of the food chain, as we'll point out in several other expense areas.)

3. If you purchase used equipment from a supplier you can plan on paying approximately half the cost of new equipment. This option will often get you a limited warranty and you'll be able to bargain on the price and options like delivery and setup.

4. Buying used equipment from a private party will cost you somewhere between 10 percent and 40 percent of the cost of new equipment, depending on the condition. This option will also give you the greatest bargaining power but, unless you know a lot about the

equipment, you might have to hire someone knowledgeable enough to inspect everything and give you a condition report. You will also have to deal with arranging to have it disconnected, moved and set up.

5.   Renting, leasing or renting with an option to buy should only be used as a temporary measure to secure equipment or if there is only a short term need for it. These options are very expensive over the long term and you will usually have little to no bargaining power.

Exercise

The purpose of this exercise is to help you get smart. Nothing more. Nothing less. So:

Make a list of the equipment you think you'll need for your business. For some businesses, this can be extensive. Also, you may not know exactly what you need. If that's the case we suggest you hunt around on the Internet to get smart. Better yet, find someone already in the business, become friends with them, ask for their advice and to help you with your list. A tour with them pointing out each piece of equipment would not hurt either.

List in hand, start hunting on the Internet for pricing. You're looking for prices for new, slightly used and "as is" equipment. Don't worry about things like the seller says it 102-years-old but in perfect condition. Or that it's located in Madagascar and shipping is going to cost ten times as much as the item. At this point, all we're trying to do is establish a "price range" for each item so we don't look totally stupid or poop our pants when we find out one item is more than our entire budget.

Notes

Chapter 11 – Property and Expenses

Property - Buy, Rent or Lease

Authors' note: In the following sections, when we talk about "property" we are referring to developed property, i.e. access and all utilities available and buildings already located on the property. If you're thinking of purchasing undeveloped property, many of the same things we cover will apply, with the added expense of constructing buildings, providing access and having utilities run to the property, which we will not cover.

***

Eeeny, meeny, miny, moe! Should I rent, lease or should I buy?

Each has advantages and each has disadvantages. Sometimes you may not have a choice, but it still pays to know what each offers and it may come in handy when you're negotiating a purchase, lease or rent.

Buying

If you can afford it, purchasing your business property gives you the most freedom and has several financial and other advantages.

Obviously, if you buy, you will not have a landlord to deal with when you want to make changes.

However, if you borrow to purchase the property, most commercial property loans will require that you pull all the necessary permits and submit the construction and finance plans to the lien holder and obtain their approval before making any improvements.

This ensures them that the changes will increase (rather than decrease) the property value or appeal and that you are able to pay for the changes.

When you own the property, your monthly mortgage payment may be less or more than if you rented or leased. The comparison between buying and renting will depend on the area, its popularity and the local economic conditions. In high demand areas, rents and leases will often be higher than loan payments, especially when the economy is good and growing.

If your considering making an offer on a piece of property, it never hurts to check what rents for similar properties are going for, even if you only use that information for leverage during price negotiations. Then too, it's nice information to have if you should need to rent or lease out your property at some time in the future.

Remember, we're dealing with income property here, not a house or residence. That means many different factors about the property (often the exact opposite of what you would look for in residential property) will come into play. For example:

- Is it highly visible and in a high traffic area?
- Are there other businesses close by to help attract customers?
- What is the surrounding neighborhood environment like?
    - o Typical income levels and product appeal consistent with your business?
    - o Schools close by, with kids hanging around the store fronts?
    - o Low income tenement housing with homeless and gang issues?

- If it's not already set up for a business identical to yours, how difficult will it be to install everything?

  - Is the space big enough to hold the equipment and supplies you need?
  - Are all the utilities you need (gas, power, plumbing, water, etc.) available and in the right places?
  - Are delivery and waste facilities available and convenient?
  - How hard and expensive will it be to install or move things to where you'd like them?

- Are support facilities available and close by?

  - USPS, UPS and Fed-X pickup and delivery.
  - Shipping companies.
  - Trash pickup.
  - IT, phone and internet service.
  - Supply stores close by.

Of course, all of these factors will apply to the property in general, whether you buy, rent or lease. However, if you buy the property you're pretty much stuck there so make sure you investigate everything you'll need before you decide to purchase. If something is unavailable, make sure your business can survive without it.

If you purchase the property and building you will have to come up with a down payment. You'll also be the one responsible for paying property taxes, and any special assessments which are often imposed on commercial property.

Finally, make sure the area is zoned and approved for your type of business. For example; often bars, strip clubs and marijuana sales require special zoning and are not allowed within so many feet of a school, church or residential area.

Rent or Lease

Renting and leasing basically mean the same thing. You're paying to use someone else's property.

The two things that typically differentiate renting from leasing are, the length of time you commit to rent the property, and the terms of the rental contract.

A lease implies a longer term commitment to rent the property, often a year or more, where as a rental agreement typically implies month-to-month. With a lease agreement not only are you committing to staying in that place for the specified time period, you're also agreeing to a fixed amount of rent every month for the duration of the lease.

Leasing

On the minus side, with a lease you're committing to rent the property for an extended amount of time, e.g. one or more years. On the plus side, your rent is fixed for that period of time.

Because a lease agreement guarantees you'll occupy the property for an extended amount of time, lease agreements are often much more flexible in terms of changes and additions you're permitted to make to the property. Here again though, often approval from the owner or leasing agent is required before you can go ahead with the changes.

One last minus on the side of a lease is that more often than not, you'll be responsible for any maintenance and upkeep on the premises you're leasing.

Renting

With rent, you're usually committed to a much shorter period of time, typically one month. In addition, your rent is fixed only for that month and can be raised at the end of each month.

Additionally, because there is no guarantee for how long you'll occupy the property, there are often much stricter rules on letting you make changes.

On the plus side, maintenance and upkeep is usually the responsibility of the property owner.

However, all that may be moot because finding commercial property for rent on a month to month basis is often difficult, if not impossible. Again, we're not talking about residential property where a landlord can find a new renter quickly. Thus, commercial property owners want to be assured that their property will produce income for as long as possible and with as little effort on their part as possible. And that implies a lease.

Utilities

Public Utilities

Standard public utilities include gas or propane, electric, water, sewage and trash. Whether you rent, lease or buy, these should be put in your or your business name.

Why, you ask?

For several reasons. First, if something happens, such as a gas leak, a water line break or an electricity blackout, you're the one you'll want them to contact. If you rent or lease, it's okay to list the owner or property manager as a backup person to call as long as they have access to the property and buildings, but you should be the primary point of contact.

Additionally, you'll want to be the one receiving any notices, such as rate increases or scheduled outages

Second, utility rates can vary with the type of business and for some businesses, utility companies may even offer a special discount. Also, if you're a high consumption user often you can receive special rates.

Finally, if the health or wellbeing of humans or animals depends on a utilities' reliability, you can have your business listed as "critical to restore" should there be an outage or blackout.

Examples of this might be our friend with the horse rescue ranch, a home health care service provider and any type of medical facility.

Privately Provided Utilities

Today, most communications related utilities (phone, cable and Internet service) are provided by multiple private companies vying for your business.

The two key factors in selecting which provider to use should be cost and reliability. Often the lower cost provider may be able to offer those cheap rates because they skimp on repair staff and equipment. That means when you lose Internet service it may be days before it gets restored.

Here again, we'll remind you this is your business and not being able to process credit cards for two days means you may as well shut down till the Internet comes back up. So consider all factors and choose wisely.

Equipment Set up and Decorating

Unless you've purchased a going business identical to yours with everything already in place, you'll have to set up your business location with everything you need. This can range from building a new structure, installing new equipment or simply moving things around. No matter which of these you fall under, there is planning and expenses related to setting up your business.

Using your equipment list from the previous chapter, sketch out where you think each piece of equipment needs to go, including furniture. This will give you some idea of how much space you'll need and whether or not locations you're considering will work.

Don't forget to think about work flow, utility connections, lighting, storage space, shipping and receiving of goods, etc. If your business is production oriented, you'll likely want to hire someone with production line set up experience to do this for you. If all you need is office space, you can likely do this yourself.

Don't forget to look at restroom accommodations.

- Are there enough? Male/Female/Unisex.
- Are they handicap accessible?
- In good condition or do they need new fixtures and/or reconditioning?

Finally, list any decorative or other items you'll need to install.

- Reception station or desk.
- Retaining and full walls.
- Blinds.
- Signage.
- Paint (or paint changes).
- Carpeting/tile and wood flooring.

- Coffee station with utility sink.
- Handicap accommodations and parking.
- Shelving, cabinetry and other fixtures.
- Repairs.

Payroll

Once you've decided on a payroll system, how many employees you'll have, and what benefits you'll provide, you'll need to set up your payroll system.

Your payroll system should tie into your bookkeeping system, but be sure the system(s) you choose have proper security barriers and access features to protect and prevent unauthorized access to employee information. (See Chapter 9 Accounting and Bookkeeping.)

You'll also want to make sure your payroll system generates all of the necessary withholding and tax forms. (See Chapter 12 Taxes.)

Insurance

Be sure to provide for the various types of insurance expense your business will need and what you provide for your employees. (See Chapter 15 Insurance.)

Summary

This chapter points out as many of the typical expenses that your business might incur. Is it a complete list? No.

Obviously expenses will vary from business to business and property may not be a factor in some.

Exercise

Make a list of the expenses you think your business will incur. Some of these may be one-time expenses as you set up your business, others may be monthly or even weekly.

Once your accounting and bookkeeping systems are in place, make sure they accommodate all of the expenses on your list. Likewise, check to see if your systems all integrate well and calculate items important to your knowing how your business is doing, i.e. cost of sales, profit margin per product, overall profit margin and so forth.

Notes

Chapter 12 – Taxes

Ah yes! Taxes! Everybody loves taxes. NOT!

We're so sorry to have to add this chapter, but it really is a must. We'll try and make it as short and painless as possible and you might want to grab a beer, glass of wine or both before we start into it.

Much of what we talk about here can be pawned off on your accounting person. If that's you well, again we're sorry and you'll want to make that two bottles of beer and/ or glasses of wine.

When you choose your accounting and bookkeeping systems, taxes should be one of your main concerns. Just some of the taxes you'll need your system to track and calculate for you will be:

- Property.
- Sales.
- Payroll.
- Alcohol.
- Special taxes unique to your business.

Most good accounting systems will be designed to accommodate these and other common business related taxes. Make sure there are also provisions to add special taxes, e.g. foreign taxes and tariffs, add on local sales taxes, special payroll withholding and other taxes unique to your business or area.

Business and Employee Tax Forms

In addition to accommodating the various taxes imposed on your business, the system you choose should be capable of generating a variety of standard business and employee related tax forms.

Here again, make sure the system you choose has enough flexibility to handle all your needs with room to spare. You'll also want to make sure that creating new forms or tracking selected taxes is easy to understand and implement and doesn't take a rocket scientist with and accounting degree to master. (Or should that be a master's degree in accounting and rocket science?)

Depreciation

As the assets owned by your business age, their usefulness, and therefore their value, becomes less and less as they reach their expected life span. This is called depreciation.

For businesses, depreciation comes in two forms: Long term depreciation for assets expected to retain their usefulness over a long period of time, typically over 50 years, and short term depreciation for equipment assets with a useful life of around 5 years or less.

Note that the definitions of long and short term depreciations can vary widely, depending on which government agency you're dealing with and who's calculating them, and why.

Short Term Depreciation

Examples of short term depreciation items may be a stove or refrigerator in a restaurant, an office desk or furniture, hand and small power tools, desk top computers and printers.

Items that fall under short term depreciation are usually devalued using a straight line equation and are considered to be valueless at the end of their depreciation term. Thus if an item is expected to last 5 years, at the end of two years its value would be 60 percent of its original value.

Long Term Depreciation

Buildings and systems that are permanently affixed to them (heating and air conditioning, water softening and filtration systems, lighting, etc.) retain their usefulness over a much longer period of time and are subject to long term depreciation

However, long term item are commonly in use more often or all day and require more and more maintenance as they approach the end of their estimated useful life. Therefore they are devalued on a curve, rather than using a straight line approach. The actual depreciation calculation will depend on the item or piece of equipment, its expected life span and its typical use.

Depreciation and Taxes

Depreciation is tied closely to taxes and each year the value of your business is affected by the devaluation of your equipment, property, inventory and other assets.

It's extremely important that you accurately enter each of your assets into your accounting and bookkeeping systems as you set your business up. From there, your system should automatically keep track of the depreciation of each item over each year of its use.

Summary

Your accounting and bookkeeping systems should accommodate and keep track of the various types of taxes imposed on your business. In addition, it should retain and calculate the depreciation of your assets for both long term and short term depreciated items.

Finally, your systems should automatically generate any and all tax related forms required by your business.

Exercise

Research and list the various taxes and tax forms that will apply to your business.

List the equipment, property and other assets you'll need in two lists: one long term depreciated items and the other, short term depreciated items.

Check each of these lists against the accounting and bookkeeping systems you want to use. Make certain the system can accommodate everything your business needs.

Remember, everything your system doesn't do for you, you'll need to do by hand or pay someone to do.

Notes

Chapter 13 - Financing

We're going to climb on our soap box and do a lot of yelling at you in this chapter so, stand warned.

Money? OMG, I need money! Maybe I should talk to my cousin Guido, he always has plenty of money! Or mom and dad, they just paid off the house and can refinance for their favorite son. Oh, I know, I'll ask my sister Grazilla and her friend Daisy Mist as soon as they get back from Florida.

There are many ways to finance your business. You can support the business with your own money, borrow from family members, friends, financial institutions or private loan sources. You can also seek grants or loans from special programs set up to encourage and support small businesses or other specialty business fields and loans available from the Veterans Administration (VA) if you've been in the military.

And just like everything else we've been banging on about: It's research, research, research! Hunt around nationally, statewide and locally. Just be sure to investigate any of them you might plan to use very carefully. First, make sure that the company or organization is legitimate. Then, negotiate an interest rate and pay off requirements that are reasonable and that you can afford.

Yes, we said negotiate! As in, don't just accept what they offer; unless of course their offer is much better than the rates you expected.

This next bit of advice may sound totally stupid, but no matter how or who you get the money from, **plan on paying it back!**

This is the business world. Money, even if it comes from your mum and dad's vacation or new car savings jar, **you're borrowing it**. And mum and dad expect it to be paid back.

Guido and his friends (especially his boss, the Godfather guy) don't want to hear how your piss poor business skills are making you lose money each month. All they know is they expect and want their money back, along with interest- usually lots of it. Besides, you'll be giving them an excuse to remove the "pond scum, piss poor, no business skills guy" from the neighborhood.

Most loan institutions can be as unsympathetic as Guido and often have zero tolerance for businesses that fail to make their loan payments. This is why many banks, credit unions and S&Ls (Savings and Loans) do not do business loans, especially to small businesses and more especially to first time small business owners. Simply put, you're too much of a risk.

Don't believe us? Go ask your bank if they offer small business loans or watch Bar Rescue or Restaurant Rescue. Actually, we suggest you do both as part of your research homework!

Banks and Lending Institutions

If you're lucky enough to find a local bank, or other lending institution, that does small business loans, plan on spending days there groveling, begging and filling out paperwork.

Banks and lending institutions will insist on you convincing them that:

1. You're a good risk.
2. You know what you're doing and will be successful.

3. You'll use their bank for any and all business accounts and get their approval on anything related to financial matters. (And not just business matters!)
4. You'll stockpile enough money in an account with them so if you have a rough month (or two or three), payments on your loan are covered.
5. You'll pledge that your first, second, and maybe even your third born, will be enslaved to pay off your loan after they reach the age of 18.
6. You'll fill out enough forms to create a roaring barn fire at every Friday night high school football game for the next year.

Oh. And just when you think you're done? They'll likely refuse your loan.

If you're one of the lucky ones and your loan is approved, they'll lay out a payment schedule for you and you will pretty much know when your payments will be due and how much they will be. In most cases they will also send you a reminder several days before your payment date followed by a very nasty note if you miss the payment.

Miss two payments and they'll expect your first born on their doorstep the next morning.

As noted, many banks will insist that you maintain your business, and sometimes your personal, accounts with them. This is not because they are nice! This is because you're using their money and they want to make sure they get it back. And what better way to make sure that happens than to hold ALL of your money.

Is that bad? Yes and no.

If you plan on not repaying them or only making your payments when:

- You feel like it.

- Snicker Doodle, your 90-to-1 horse in the second race, wins.
- When your business finally makes a profit.
- Your wife/husband/mate hasn't spent everything you've got.

Then a bank loan is probably not for you. Actually, no legal source of money is probably going to work for you. Nor will you likely be in business for very long.

Seriously folks, it bears repeating: Money isn't free. No matter where it comes from, they expect repayment and some form of interest.

And remember, if you borrowed from cousin Guido and his shady friends, and you value your ability to walk from one place to another, you either need to make sure you have a secret stash or hide those plane tickets (and the raft for the last 10 or so miles) to Koh Yao Noi Island in Thailand.

One last thing, if you do apply for a bank, S&L, SBA (Small Business Association) or other commercial institution that offers loans, you'll find that doing many of the things we've suggested in our book will be of tremendous help in securing a loan.

Why? Because what we're telling you need to do is exactly what they want to know; that you've done your homework. That you know what you're getting into and have planned things out. Not only if things fall into place and you're successful, but also if they don't and you have to go to plan B or plan C. More importantly, that you have a plan B and plan C!

Finally, many of the things we have you doing in the exercises will make filling out the tons of forms simple by putting the raft of the information they'll want at your fingertips.

While were on banks. Whenever you're dealing with a bank for loans, accounts, or anything else, be sure to tell them if you're a veteran. In addition to the sources and benefits noted below, almost all banks offer special accounts or special rates and privileges to those who have served their country.

Other Loan Sources

Military Service Related Loans with Special Rates and Benefits

Are you a veteran? Check with your local Veterans Administration (VA) office to see what kinds of small business loans and or grants they offer.

These programs, set up by the government, often offer special interest rates and payback provisions that have a much lower interest rate and more lenient terms than anything commercial banks or institutions offer.

But don't stop there. Check with the branch of service you served in. Often specific branches of the military also offer loans, or more likely grants, that don't go through the VA. Because these are grants, there is no interest or payback requirement. However, the amount available under a grant program will likely be much less than that under a loan program.

Are you the spouse of a veteran? The child of a deceased veteran or a service member killed while on active duty? Here again, the VA and/or a specific branch of service may offer loans specifically to help spouses and family members start or sustain a small business.

A word of caution!

Be extremely careful! There are a ton of people and loan organizations out there who advertise they offer loans to veterans, spouses, special SBA loans for veterans, loans for crippled veterans, loans for Viet Nam veterans, loans for Civil War veterans, etc.

Many of these are just come-ons. The VA, or a specific military service branch, are the only ones that can offer a loan to veterans with guaranteed special rates that are backed by the government! Anyone else who says they can offer you that is full of crap.

One other thing while we're thinking of it. If anyone wants a fee up front to "process" you loan application... **Walk Away**! This is a surefire way to collect your money, let you wait several days or weeks, then conveniently turn you down. Oh, and request you resubmit, with a new fee, when things "improve" in the financial world.

Federal, State and Local Agencies

Many federal, state and local agencies offer special loans or loan packages to try and entice small businesses to open in their region, state, city or town. Often these are offered through agencies such as the local SBA or BBB (Better Business Bureau).

While the rates and provisions on these types of loans may be more attractive, typically they are offered through local lending agencies and their only benefit is "a foot in the door with the bank", so to speak. That is not to say do not explore them. Every little bit of help in securing a loan is worth looking into.

Social Organizations, Clubs and Private Loan Sources

Other places to check include the local: Kiwanis Club, Masons, 4H Club, business and civic associations, and any other place you can think of.

Sure, some of these will only deal with certain types of businesses (like only small animal related entities for the 4H Club) but, leave no stone unturned!

As you roam through the financial world, remember not only are you looking for a loan source, you're also trying to get to meet other business owners, make friends with potential customers and vendors...

As for private loans? Well, we've talked enough about borrowing from mum and dad's jar funds, other relatives and Guido and his friends, enough for you to know, you're on your own.

However, we'll repeat our one word of advice: **DON'T**

Summary

In this chapter, we've covered traditional, non-traditional and specialized loan sources.

We've also tried to give you some idea of where to look for loans and grants, what to expect from each and tried to provide some tips and precautions.

Exercise

If you need to borrow money to get your business started, or you want to be prepared in case you might need a business loan in the future, we suggest you do the following:

- Go to your bank and ask to speak with a loan advisor. Even if your bank does not offer business loans, their loan advisor is often an excellent source of information and advice and can likely point you to banks that do offer small business loans.

- While you're there, ask for a business loan application or a list of information you'd need to submit on a loan application. Look over the list and make sure you have everything you'll need. Also, be aware that loan applications vary from bank to bank and loan type to loan type so be sure to prepare a list of secondary information that you think might be on another application.

- Research small business loan sources on the internet. Start with the SBA, but also check other local and regional sources. (BBB, social organizations, etc.) Don't forget to look for grants sources too. These can be extremely helpful if some time in the future you need a limited amount of money to carry your business through a down period.

- If you're a veteran, or relative of a veteran, check with the VA or the closest charity/service veteran and family support office for your branch of the military, e.g. the Navy Marine Corp Relief Society (NMCRS), Air Force Aid Society (AFAS), GoArmy or Coast Guard Mutual Assistance (CGMA).

One final note. We can't emphasize enough to thoroughly investigate any loan source and their loan conditions! Yes, even the banks. Make sure they are not only reputable but that you completely understand the terms and conditions of the loan or grant they are offering. Remember, even the large banks, such as Bank of America, Wells Fargo, Citibank and Chase, might offer high risk loans, but with terms that may be totally unacceptable to you.

Notes

Chapter 14 - Licenses, Permits and Registration

We probably should have said this sooner, but much of the technical things we're telling you can be found on the government's Small Business Administration (SBA) web site: https://www.sba.gov. We strongly suggest you take the time to look over their website.

By the way, as mentioned in Chapter 13 Financing, the SBA is also an excellent source for small business loans. Along with that is a bunch of information on not only loans but grant sources and what type of information you'll need to provide when applying for each.

Business Licenses

License and permit requirements are going to vary depending on where you establish your business and the type of business you're starting. Also, make sure you check the requirements at the local, state and federal level for your particular business as often permits or licenses of the same or different type may be required by more than one agency.

Almost every town, city, county or state will require a general business license. Often, this may be combined with another type of license or permit, such as a seller's license/permit and, may depend on how you register your business.

Seller's Licenses, Sales Permits and Sales Taxes

Almost all businesses will require a seller's license or sales permit. However, one may be required by your local (town, city or county) agency while a separate license or permit may be required by the state. Often these are tied to a sales tax account to ensure you collect and pay sales taxes at both the local and state level.

If your business is only providing a service typically you'll only need a license such as a contractor's license. Here again, you'll need to check and see what's required for your type of business in your particular area. A lot of cities and states do not charge sales tax on services, but then, a lot do. So you need to check.

How do you find out all this? You guessed it, here we go again: Research, research, research! But, take heart. Often all of the license and permit requirements for a particular type of business will be listed on an agency's website. This will make your search a lot easier. However, more often than not, they are only going to list their requirements and not those at other levels. Here again, the SBA website is an excellent source for an overview of the requirements for most states.

But wait, you say. If I'm a plumber and I fix someone's sink, I'll need parts. So I should have to pay sales tax, right?

Yes and no. It depends. In most states the sales tax in this case would be a pass through, i.e. the supplier you buy your parts from would pay the sales tax on whatever parts they sold you. You would then simply pass that on by charging the customer whatever you paid for the parts. If you charge them more than you paid, which is typical, the added amount would be considered a service charge for stocking, transporting or ordering the parts, which may be

not be subject to sales tax: depending on your local or
state tax laws.

Types of Business Registration

Let's skip to business registration for a second since many
states and local areas tie their licensing requirements to
how you've registered your business.

Why You Need to Register

The biggest reason for registering your business is
protection (no, not from Guido), which we'll cover under
the advantages of each type of registration.

In some cases, you may not need to register at all. In some
areas and states you can simply conduct business as yourself,
using only your legal name. But remember, if you don't register
your business, you could miss out on some benefits of
registering such as, personal liability protection, legal benefits,
and tax benefits.

How do You Want to Register Your Business?

In most cases, small businesses will be registered as:

- A sole proprietorship, where you are the sole owner.
- A partnership, where several people, as partners,
  own the business.
- A Limited Partnership (LP), where you take on
  partners but maintain control.
- An LLP Partnership or LLC Corporation, a Limited
  Liability Partnership or Corporation.
- Or, possibly a Chapter C or S Corporation.

What Are the Advantages and Disadvantages of Each?

Sole Proprietorship – A sole proprietorship means you are the sole owner of the business. This means you have complete control over all aspects of the business.

The main advantages of a sole proprietorship, aside from having complete control, are; it's easy to form and register and, from a tax standpoint your business assets become part of your personal assets. That is, they are not considered separate, even though they'll be listed separately and treated differently on your tax forms.

If you live in an area where you do not need to register your business, you'll automatically be considered as a sole proprietorship if you do business activities but don't register as any other kind of business.

However, a sole proprietorship does not produce a separate business entity, even if you obtain a trade (business) name. This means your business assets and liabilities are not separate from your personal assets and liabilities. Thus, you can be held personally liable for the debts and obligations of the business, which puts your personal assets at risk.

A sole proprietorship can also make it hard to raise money. Typically, banks are hesitant to lend to sole proprietorships. You also can't sell shares or stock in the ownership of your business without changing it to some form of partnership.

While we're not sure if there is such a thing as a low risk business anymore, if you think your business is low risk or, you want to test your business before jumping in there without all the complications of a more formal business structure, a sole proprietorship may be a great way to test things out.

Partnerships – A partnership is where two or more people own a business together. The two most common forms of partnerships are: limited partnerships (LP) and limited liability partnerships (LLP).

But wait. What about a general or straight partnership you ask?

Yes, there is such a thing, however, for a small business we really do not recommend them. Here's why. In a straight partnership, everyone is a general partner. This means everyone is equal, with an equal say, equal risk and on the plus side, shares equally in the profits.

So what's wrong with all that? Well, nothing; if all the partners trust each other, share equally in the work, get along exceptionally well and are willing to compromise when you all can't reach agreement on something. Oh, and are all willing to go down with the ship if it sinks.

Get where we're going? The ship is a good analogy: It's like a ship with 2, 3, 4, or however many, captains. And, not so much "the more the merrier" as the more partners, the more complicated things get. Typically, exponentially.

Add the stress of starting a new business and often simple decisions get haggled over, friendship are stretched to their limit and, in each case the business usually suffers. Yip, ranks right up there with hiring your relatives!

Limited Partnerships (LP) – Limited partnerships solve many of the above problems by having only one general partner with unlimited liability, while all the other partners have limited liability. The limited liability partners also tend to have limited or no control over the company; all of which is defined in the partnership agreement.

Profits are also split at a percentage (typically based on the amount invested or day-to-day involvement of each partner) as defined by the agreement and paid as if the limited partners were employees.

This approach obviously defines each partners role, if any, in the business decisions and day-to-day operations, hopefully to avoid the issues raised above for a straight partnership.

A limited partnership also protects each of the limited partners from debts against the partnership or responsibility for the actions of the other partners.

Two things to keep in mind: The general partner has unlimited liability and is at risk, just as if it were his/her sole proprietorship, and the smooth operation of the business will only be as good as the terms limiting the control of each partner in the partnership agreement.

Limited Liability Partnerships (LLP) - Limited liability partnerships are similar to limited partnerships but also give limited liability to the general partner.

While this type of partnership protects the general partner, it puts all risk solely on the business and its assets.

At first, an LP or LLP may seem like they protect most or all partners from liability. However, in today's "sue everybody" world we're not sure how much protection they really offer.

In summary, partnerships can be a good choice for businesses with multiple owners. A General Partnership is often a good choice for professional groups (like attorneys), while LPs and LLPs typically work better for most small, non-professional businesses. Finally, partnerships, like sole proprietorships, can be used by groups who want to test their business idea before forming a more formal business such as a company or corporation.

Company or Limited Liability Company (LLC) - A company or LLC lets you take advantage of the benefits of both the corporation and partnership business structure. The biggest benefit is that profits and losses can be passed through to your personal income without facing corporate taxes.

However, members of a company and LLC are considered self-employed and must pay self-employment contributions to Medicare and Social Security.

Like an LLP, LLCs protect your personal assets (home, vehicles and bank accounts) from personal liability in most instances if your LLC faces bankruptcy or lawsuits. But, here again, in today's sue everyone environment, an LLC doesn't assure the safety of your personal assets if you are sued separately from the company.

A word of caution. In many states, LLCs can have a limited life. Often, if a member joins or leaves an LLC, some states may require the LLC be dissolved and re-formed with the new membership. This can be avoided, however, by putting in place an agreement within the LLC that provides for buying, selling, and transferring ownership.

If the business you're opening is either medium or high risk, a corporation or LLCs can be a good choice. If the owners have significant personal assets that they want to protect, an LLC would be a better option. An added benefit in either case would be a lower tax rate than they would pay with a corporation.

Corporations - A corporation is a legal entity that's separate from its owners. While corporations offer the best protection from personal liability, they are extremely complex and expensive to form. Aside from personal liability protection, a corporation also has the advantage of being able to raise capital through the sale of stock. However, by law, they require extensive record keeping and reporting systems, as well as formal operational procedures.

There are also multiple types of corporations, each with their own unique advantages, disadvantages, complexities and regulation requirements.

Registering as a corporation is typically beyond the realm of most small businesses; especially a new or start up small business. If you'd like further information on corporations, we suggest you check the SBA website which has an excellent overview description of each type, along with its major advantages and disadvantages.

If you're seriously thinking of setting up a corporation, we strongly advise that you start by seeking the advice of a corporate attorney.

Joint Ventures - Another term you'll likely come across is a joint venture. A joint venture, however, is not a recognized business structure. It is simply an agreement typically between two companies to jointly work on (and often fund) a particular project.

***

Business Unique Licenses and Permits

License and permit requirements for various businesses vary all over the place. Some are obvious, such as a liquor or alcohol license for a bar or restaurant, but others are not, like a

Controlled Substance Permit for each employee that works in a veterinarian's office.

Permits issued by the Health Department are also typically required for businesses such as bars, restaurants, medical facilities, and even a produce stand at the local farmers' market.

Our advice: Once you've selected a business structure and have a good idea about location, check the Internet for registration, license and permit requirements for the town, city, county, state and federal governments.

Remember that the ownership rules, liability, taxes, and filing requirements for each business type varies not only from state to state but from county to county and often town to town. So don't assume that what's required in your area is the same on the other side of the county line.

Summary

In this chapter we've explained the different ways you can register your business, along with the major advantages and disadvantages of each. We also touched on some of the more common types of business licenses and permits that would typically apply to most small businesses.

Finally, we've tried to give you some idea of how these will vary from state to state, city to city, town to town, county to county and agency to agency.

Exercise

- Go to the SBA or other websites that define business registration and look over the different ways to register your business. Pick the one that you think would best serve your business.

- Next, look up what you'll need to do to register your business and related licensing and permit requirements for your type of business and potential location. This should include researching the requirements at the town, city, county and state level. Make sure you check all of them as often each will have their own unique requirements.

- Make a list of the licenses and permits you'll need, how and where to obtain each and how and where to register. Make sure you look up and have handy all of the information you'll need to apply for each of them.

In most cases, applying for whatever you need can easily be done on-line. However, be aware that often things like a liquor license or a Health Department permit may require an extensive background check or an inspection of your business location.

Likewise, in the case of a liquor license, many states and municipalities limit the number of licenses allowed in a given area. So be sure and check to make sure what you need is available or that you can be put on a waiting list.

Notes

Chapter 15 - Insurance

Businesses require all types of insurance. We'll try and cover the types of insurance common to most businesses. We'll also point out riders and supplemental insurance that we're aware of or that may pertain to certain business types or situations.

We've also tried to list them in their order of importance, as we see it.

Finally, if your personal insurance is through a company that provides business insurance (State Farm, Allstate, Farmers, USAA) we suggest you give them a call and talk to an agent. Explain what type of business you're opening and ask for their help and recommendations. This will give you a base to start down the twisty turny road of investigating each type of insurance you'll need.

Liability Insurance

No matter how you've listed your business, liability is still one of the biggest threats to any business. In today's *sue everybody* world, being an LLC, LLP, or limited liability anything else, does not prevent someone from suing you, as well as your business.

Simply stated, if a business with limited liability is sued, then the claimants are suing the company, not its owners or investors. A shareholder in a limited company, or the limited partners in a limited partnership, are not personally liable for any of the debts of the company, other than for the amount already invested in the company and for any unpaid amount on the shares in the company, if any.

But while the limited liability may limit your liability in a suit against the company, it does not prevent anyone from suing you as an individual.

Let's see if we can come up with an easy to understand example.

One of your customers leaves your store, turns left, trips over a shopping cart someone left there and falls. In doing so, they break their arm in three places, fracture their cheek and break their nose.

The following week, you receive notice of two law suits. One against the business and one against you.

The suit against the business alleges that it is the business' responsibility to keep the walkway in front of your store free from hazards, such as shopping carts.

The suit against you alleges that it is your responsibility to see that employees do cart round-ups to keep the walkway and parking area clear of such hazards and obviously you failed to do so or they would not have tripped over the cart.

While you may laugh or shake your head at our example, we believe it is unfortunately very close to what happens far too often.

So our recommendation is that you not only make sure you have liability insurance for your business but also for yourself. This can be in the form of a separate policy or part of an umbrella policy as defined further in this section.

Damage, Fire, Flood and Loss

Fire

Insurance against common business hazards include fire, flood, loss and damage.

Fire and flood insurance may seem to be pretty straight forward but once again, this is your business, your livelihood, so you really need to pay attention to the fine print.

First, make sure your coverage is for full replacement value of all damage and lost items. Paying only 80 percent of the assessed cost to repair damage leaves you scraping up the other 20 percent, and often, while your business remains closed during the repairs.

Also look to see if there's a provision limiting the time before your claim is settled. If not, try to negotiate a partial payment(s) clause so you can get started with clean up and repairs while the company haggles over what they're going to pay out and who they want to make the repairs.

Finally, make sure replacement of your stock is fully covered too. Under your fire insurance, not just for fire damage but for smoke and water damage also. Often putting the fire out causes more damage than the actual fire itself. And don't forget about coverage for those items no one will want because they smell like smoked salmon, unless of course it is smoked salmon. Then, feel free to mark it up and sell it on super special as "double smoked salmon".

Flood

No matter where your business is located, pay particular attention to your flood insurance. Outdated maps can put your property in a flood zone when it is not, or not put you in one when you in fact are. Either way, this will have a major impact on the cost of your flood insurance. (See, The Flood Insurance Merry-go-round in Part 3, Stories.)

The first thing we will tell you is that flood insurance is one of the most confusing insurance policies you'll likely have to deal with. It will probably be one of the most expensive too.

With global warming (Uh sorry, "just weather" according to President Trump) and the rash of storms and resulting floods and mud slides they've caused, no place is safe. Even if you're on top of a hill. Actually, with mud slides, **especially** if you're on top of a hill.

It used to be that a trip to the county recorder's office was called for to find out if you were in a flood plain before you looked into flood insurance. However, in today's crazy climate world, we recommend you look into obtaining flood insurance, no matter where you're located.

If you can afford it, there are several things to make sure your policies cover. First, mudslides as well as floods. Second, water and mud damage to your products as well as your property and structures. Also, see if you have or can negotiate a minimum payout time or progressive payments to allow cleanup and the start of repairs while your total claim is settled.

Finally, if complete insurance is impossibly expensive, look at a reduced coverage policy. Remember, something is better than nothing and reduced coverage may at least help you start getting your business back open or give you a down payment for a new location.

Damage and Loss

Depending on the insurance company, damage and loss may be covered under another type of policy, such as an Umbrella Policy or under one or more separate policies or riders.

Damage and loss, as we define them here, could be caused by any number of events beyond your control. A runaway vehicle slamming into your building. Vandalism and/or theft. Employee theft. Accidental spillage. Spoilage. Equipment failure.

No matter how the coverage is provided, try to make sure your policy covers every possible cause you can think of. In many cases, this will also be dependent on the type of business you operate.

For example: If your restaurant's walk-in refrigerator stops working over a holiday weekend when you're closed and everything in it spoils, make sure you're covered under one policy or another. Whether it was caused by vandalism or the compressor breaking down, you'll want to be reimbursed so you can replace the items and get back to cooking wonderful meals.

Special Policies or Riders (Umbrella Policies, Earthquake and Tornado Insurance)

Umbrella Policies

An Umbrella insurance Policy provides liability insurance that is in excess of other policies. It also provides insurance in excess of primary insurance for losses not covered by the other policies. If an insured is covered by an umbrella policy and is found liable, the insured's primary insurance policies pay up to their limits, and any additional amount is paid by the umbrella policy, up to the limit of the umbrella policy.

Put into plain English: your primary policy will pay out first, up to its' limit. Then the umbrella policy will pay any additional amount, up to its' limit.

Umbrella coverage for insurance other than liability will vary from company to company so shop around to make sure you can find the coverage you want.

Earthquake and Tornado Insurance

Insurance coverage for earthquakes or tornados will obviously depend on where your business is located. These often come in the form of riders, which are added to your existing property insurance.

Taking out earthquake Insurance in New York would probably be a waste of money. But if your business is in New York and you want to be super protected, be aware that there have been 395 earthquake incidents in New York since 1931 and the state averages 5 earthquakes per year. None of them, however, have been very large nor have they caused much damage. So, save your money.

Tornados, however, are a different story. While not coming close to Oklahoma, New York has its fair share of tornados every year. So in either state, New York, Oklahoma, and many others, you might want to investigate getting tornado coverage.

Vehicle Insurance

If you have one or more vehicles that are dedicated to the business, it makes sense to insure them on a separate policy under the business name.

While it is not uncommon for small business owners or even employees to use their personal vehicle for business, for your sake and theirs, you should check with your auto insurance carrier and make sure you and they are covered in case of an accident.

This is especially important when it comes to liability. Again, we'll remind you of the hundreds of sue happy people out there who will picture you and your business as having deep pockets. Thus, be honest with your agent or carrier and discuss the best approach to coverage with them.

Medical and Dental Insurance

Yay! You just became, or are about to become, a business owner! Party time! Break out the beer, wine, party favors and balloons!

Oops, wait a minute. I lost my medical and dental insurance when I left my job in search of my dream of opening my own business. Holy crap! Now what?

Fear not, buckaroo! There are hundreds of plans and programs out there. Actually, if you have employees, that gives you the opportunity to consider a group policy. Not only will that typically provide coverage at a lower cost per person, it will also allow your employees to opt in for coverage and allow you several options:

- Coverage you provide for them as an employee benefit.

- Coverage where the cost is split between you and them.
- Coverage they pay for but at a lower price because of the group policy.

No matter which option you choose, having medical and dental coverage available is a major attraction to any potential employee.

If you're considering medical and dental coverage we suggest you research (There's that word again!) providers on the Internet and choose two or three that service your area. Contact them and ask them to have a representative sit down with you and go over all the available options and costs per person.

We also suggest you investigate HMO (Health Maintenance Organization) type policies. While these will limit where you can go for your medical care, an HMO policy is often much cheaper than a non-restrictive policy. However, once again do your research! Make sure the medical group has a good reputation before you commit to using only them for your health care.

As for dental care, all of the above applies to it too.

Life Insurance

If you have a business partner, or someone critical to your business, you might want to think about obtaining life insurance on them, typically referred to as "key man insurance".

Key man insurance, also known as key person or key employee insurance, is coverage which can help protect your business in the case of an untimely death or disability of someone that the business relies heavily on.

Such insurance will obviously not help you replace that person, but it will provide additional income to help you sustain your business until you find their replacement.

Summary

Each businesses' insurance needs will differ by business type, structure and location. We've tried to cover the most common forms of insurance and also provide some idea of other types of special policies you might want to look into.

No matter what your insurance needs are, we strongly recommend you start with research and then contact an agent who specializes in business insurance needs.

Exercise

Make a list of the different types of insurance you think you'll need for your business.

Research each on the Internet to find at least three companies that provide the different types of business insurance on your list. Try to obtain as much information about each company, their reputation and the policy options they offer.

Once you feel like you can discuss each type of insurance intelligently, contact an agent or each company. Ask for their recommendations, options, and try to cost out each policy as much as possible.

Notes

Chapter 16 - Existing Businesses and Franchises

To start this chapter, we're going to remind you of our story about Daisy Mist and Grazilla. They're the ones who purchased a well run, profitable bar from Maria Estella Carman Chiquita Augustine: aka Mecca.

Remember her? She's the one who moved to Florida to sell crab tacos from a beach stand in Fort Lauderdale.

The whole purpose of that story was to make you realize that no mater what business you're thinking of, there's probably someone out there who has tried it. Maybe it's only close to what you're thinking of doing. Maybe they were successful or maybe they failed. No matter what, if you purchase their business, open or closed, it provides a major head start for you.

Like Daisy Mist and Grazilla, where Mecca left them with everything they needed to be successful (great staff, a plethora of happy, longtime customers, her recipes for great tropical style drinks and a set of books defining everything they needed to know and do to keep the business running smoothly) perhaps you can find your business for sale. One where someone is tired of running it, looking for a change, moving to a new city or state, and wants to try a different type of business, like Mecca.

By the way, we're deliberately repeating a lot from that story with the hope that you'll notice what they inherited when they purchased the business:

- A great staff.
- A plethora of happy, longtime customers.
- Her recipes for great tropical style drinks.

- A set of books defining everything they needed to know.

And honestly, a lot more, like:

- Equipment.
- Furniture.
- Decorations.
- Signage.
- Suppliers and accounts in place.

Each of these are things they would have had to do or build from scratch for their new business. So buying a successful business that's close to yours can have numerous benefits.

But what about a business that went broke, failed or never even got off the ground?

This is where we'll remind you of the old phrase, "Something is better than nothing." Failed, unpopular and even businesses with a seedy reputation can still have major benefits to a new owner. While you might not get the great staff, happy customers, menus or any books at all, there is still a lot to be gained by buying a failed business.

First of all, you will automatically have a ton of leverage during negotiations when making an offer for the business. Chances are good that if the owner's business failed, they are anxious to get rid of it, have little idea of its value or both. That truly gives you the upper hand, along with a lot of reasons to point to for not paying their asking price.

(Authors' note: We're not suggesting you screw the person selling the business. We are, however, reminding you that this is a **business** deal, not a charity event. Also, that every extra dollar you pay them for their business, is one dollar less that you have to fix up and undo their mistakes.)

As with the purchase of a going business, a failed business can also provide:

- Equipment.
- Furniture.
- Decorations.
- Signage.
- Suppliers and accounts in place.

Depending on the condition of the property and how long it's been closed.

Ah, but what about that seedy reputation? How do we change the really bad public image the place has?

Let's start with - the longer the place is closed, the more people will realize the seedy place no longer exists, especially if they see crews renovating and redecorating it day after day. Not only will that help them forget, it'll make them curious about what you're doing and what the new business will be like.

By the way, keeping it closed for a while, if it wasn't closed already, is usually not a problem given the renovations and decorating you'll likely want or have to do.

Finally, as part of your changes, you'll probably want to rebrand the business, even if it had been successful. And along with the rebranding comes a new image! The one you want them to see!

Good Will

If you buy an existing or defunct business, you'll very likely run into the term good will. Simply put, good will is the reputation that the previous owner claims to have built and has tried to put a value on. Frankly, we consider good will, along with the existing customer base if any, to have no value to the new owner.

Why? Because the reputation of a business and its customer base can disappear, and often does, the minute a business is sold. Also remember, good will is based on the way the previous owner ran their business, not the way you might run yours.

So, if you're willing for pay for good will, be prepared to have a plan in place from day one to maintain it.

Franchises

If the business world is new to you, you might want to try looking into franchise opportunities. Typically, franchises are expensive and much less flexible. Not only do they require a lot of upfront money, you run the business to their rules.

The good news is that they provide a business package with everything you need. Products, suppliers, recipes, operating procedures, advertising, building set-up, equipment, employee training and almost everything else you can think of.

Does this mean you're not going to fail? NO!

Some are good and will train you and help you. Others are not so good. They'll take your money, give you a set of rules and you'll seldom or never hear from them. Others are somewhere in between.

No matter what though, it's your business to make successful or flush down the toilet.

Summary

Purchasing an existing business, whether successful or not, can have a lot of advantages. Likewise, a franchise, if available, can also be extremely beneficial to someone new to the business world.

Exercise

Once you've completed your business plan and have an idea of where you want to open (city, state, etc), research on-line and in newspapers for businesses for sale.

You might also want to find a local real estate office that deals in selling businesses and let them know what you're looking for and what areas are acceptable to you.

Finally, if franchises are offered in your type of business, you might want to take the time to look into them.

Even if you decide they're just not for you, the list of what they provide may make a great check list so you make sure you've covered everything.

Notes

Chapter 17 - Credit Cards/POS Systems

Ah yes. Another short chapter. One that's more of a reminder and for your information than specific instructions.

In today's world, accepting credit (and debit) cards is a must, no matter what kind of business you're in.

Also, in today's world, there are multiple options that allow you to process orders and sales at the transaction site, commonly referred to as Point of Sale or POS. The old days of collecting a credit or debit card, marching over to the cash register and having a cashier process the transaction, or calling the sale in somewhere, are pretty much gone. (Yeah, we know, we just dated ourselves. Call a sale in? What does that even mean?)

Now, the sales or waitperson carries a tablet or POS terminal with them. In many cases they will enter your order into it and that will immediately be transmitted to the stock room to be filled or, in the case of a restaurant or bar that serves food, to the kitchen.

While your order is being filled, often the sales or waitperson will process your payment on the same terminal. Thus, as soon as your order is filled and handed to you, you're on your way.

These same terminals can also be tied into your inventory and ordering system therefore recording the sale, processing payment, having the item pulled from stock, reducing inventory and adding a replacement item to the next stock order.

In today's cash-free society, even businesses that don't have their own "physical place", like Bob and Robyn's book sales at a book signing, still need to be able to process credit or debit cards. Here again, there are several options for processing sales.

The most commonly used is a card swiper or chip reader that plugs into your smart phone. Two of the most common are Square and PayPal, but there are dozens out there; along with dozens of fine print fees and provisos. So, research, research, research and choose wisely for your business type.

If the amount and type of business you do warrants it, you can also use a tablet as your terminal.

Summary

There are a wide variety of POS tools and systems available for processing orders and credit card sales. These range from simple card swipers that plug into your smart phone to tablet terminals that allow you to take orders, process credit cards and tie into your inventory and ordering systems.

Exercise

List the types of functions you'd like your POS system to do.

From that list, decide if a card swiper or tablet would best suit your needs.

From there it's going to be research, research, research. Some things to be sure to look at:

- Can you tie it to your existing bank accounts or do they require a separate account? e.g. a business account if you only have a personal account.
- Easy to understand instructions for both set up and use.

- Fees. For all types of credit cards. (Remember, you don't control what kind of card a customer wants to use and the fees can vary widely by card type.)
- Amount of transactions the fee structure is based on (Often the lower fees require an extensive number of transactions per week, month or year.)
- Size and capability that fits with your employees use and your company needs.

Notes

Chapter 18 - Keeping Your Business Fresh

There supposedly was a rule in the restaurant business that you needed to completely change your menu every three years to keep your business fresh. Over the years, that has been stretched to "completely change your restaurant's image".

Many of you know this as rebranding and it has now been applied to all types of businesses, even large corporations.

Often this may follow some type of event or law suit that the company doesn't want to be associated with or doesn't want their name to be a reminder.

However, many businesses use this technique to try and stay fresh, keep up with the times and current trends.

The value of doing this can be questioned and often rebranding, or even changing something as simple as your menu, cannot only become expensive but cause you to lose customers. Like the family that comes in every Friday night for that spaghetti pizza you invented (?) and that they can't get anywhere else.

Our advice to staying fresh is simple: change what needs to be changed and keep what your customers love. More often than not, you don't need to **totally reinvent the business**, you simply need to refresh things.

That may include some things you hadn't thought of.

First and foremost, step outside and take a good look at your business. Walk down the street and come back. (If you run a non-storefront business you'll need to modify this to fit your business type.)

- Is the image you see attractive and current?

- Would you know what you sell or do based on what you see?
- Does your color scheme, frontage, signage, do everything you want it to?
- Step inside. Did your employees notice and acknowledge you? Start to offer help?

Follow the trends in your business sector, but don't just look at what others are changing.

- Look at what's successful and what's not.
- What appears to be bringing in new business.
- What are the reviews telling you? What do customers like and not like?

Set new trends

- Look at your competitors. What's missing from their products and services offering? (free DIY help and incidentals with purchased products).
- Bring back popular products and services from the past (windshield clean and oil check with each fill up).

Poll or survey your customers (Survey Monkey, and several others, offer a great way to do surveys on line after a sale.)

- Run your ideas by them (Here's a draft of our proposed new menu. What do you think?)
- Ask them what they want, what they think you should do. (Wow. Replacing the strawberry-mushroom burrito with a margarita burrito is a great idea!)
- Let them sample new things you're thinking of (Yip, stand out front and let them sample your new dish!)
- Show them your new logo, color scheme, signage and ask if they think it's more attractive, adds freshness, retains or improves your businesses image and identity. (Don't you think our new casket colors are just to die for?)

Let's look at some of the things to be careful of. Some of the biggest disasters in refreshing a business we can think of include:

Expanding – Growing beyond your knowledge and control.

- Expanding the products and footprint of your business but not taking on new employees or gaining new product knowledge and your sales and service goes down the toilet. (Adding the latest Fugi Moto Hyper Flush toilets with a built-in ass blaster wash system and TP dispenser.)
- Opening new stores/branches where you have no control over the products, service or anything else.

Rebranding – Unintentionally changing your image or losing your identity.

- Updating or changing your brand name, logo or products and resetting your expertise image back to zero. (Turning Guido's Italian Restaurant into Tembo's Pun Jab Thai Restaurant.)
- Trying to keep up with the latest trends that only last several months, maybe years if you're lucky. (Changing Guido's menu to include Italian Fusion and dry ice fused salads.)

Changing Location – Moving to a location to save on expenses

- Losing your following. (Moving to a new location beyond the limits of how far your good customers are willing to travel.)
- Moving to a location where there is little desire for your products or services. (Moving your pork BBQ slider stand to a predominately Jewish neighborhood.)

Summary

There are multiple ways to keep your business fresh including various ways to rebrand your business, but be careful not to reinvent your business, unless that is your intent.

Exercise

Look over some of the options and suggestions listed above and list those that you might want to try to keep your business fresh.

Remember though, nothing says you need to refresh, rebrand or reinvent your business. What, if anything, you do is up to you and we seriously suggest you talk to your customers and get their input before you decide to do anything. Just remember, anything you do is for them.

Notes

Part 2 – The People Side of Things

Chapter 19 – Personalities

We're going to start this part off with me (Robyn) defining the major personality types. Why? Because Part 2 deals with people and dealing with people means understanding and dealing with personalities.

Yeah, bet you never thought you'd need to know all this stuff. But we think it'll soon become apparent that personalities are critical to figuring out who you should hire, who fits where, who is management material and who is not going to fit anywhere within your business.

Understanding personalities is also important when dealing with your customers, especially the fussy ones, which we think is pretty much all of them, including us.

Finally, if you're business provides mostly services, reading and dealing with personalities will be critical to winning new customers as well as keeping your existing customers happy.

***

Studies have shown that in the workplace there will be 20 percent of people who you'll bond with, 60 percent of people you'll get on with OK and the other 20 percent are just weird (only kidding!).

Sometimes we can't figure out why someone thinks or acts in a certain way and everything would be much easier if they just thought or acted like us. Or we think *Why did that person have to be so difficult?* when it's never us who is difficult, is it?

If we understood where others were coming from we would see that people are different from us rather than just being difficult.

In business you will end up working with a multiple of personalities and it's helpful to understand what characteristics make up these personalities.

A helpful way to clarify our understanding is to do a personality test. There are a heap of them. Put 'personality tests' into Google and you'll get everything from a Star Wars personality test to The Simpsons personality test. The most respected personality test is Myers-Briggs, which is based on theory from Carl Jung. Myers-Briggs has sixteen different personality groups.

One of the more simplified versions uses four groups to show different types of personality traits.

Before you can think about what other people who you work with might be, it's important to understand what kind of personality you have.

See if you can pick what your dominant personality is from the descriptions below:

Drivers

You can tell Drivers immediately; they're busy doing stuff.

They love goals, deadlines, to do lists, and business plans. Use words like results and outcomes in their presence and their eyes will just glow!

They are the fast and the furious. Slow is not in their vocabulary. They want to get in, get on and get it done. Get out of their way or you'll get run over!

They are high achievers and have high expectations not only of themselves but others they work with.

Time is very important to a Driver. They are intolerant of time wasters, they hate waiting and they don't do queues.

Drivers like to be in control, they're strong-willed, purposeful and can sometimes be seen by others as being bossy, i.e. "It's my way or the highway."

In business they are quite often the boss, the team leader or the general manager.

The best way to work with a Driver is to be efficient.

How to influence a Driver:

- Cut to the chase - be brief, specific and to the point; provide an executive summary for written information.
- Keep to the work at hand and avoid digressions.
- Be prepared (complete all research and provide a number of solutions).
- Be clear and logical when presenting facts.
- Refer to objectives, results, outcomes and solutions.
- Show how proposals can be effectively implemented and have a positive impact on the bottom line.
- Be confident and assertive.

Oh, and avoid being hesitant or wordy, don't focus on feelings or try to take over.

Expressives

Expressives love to talk. You'll hear them before you see them. They're the life and soul of the office (hint: don't put them in an office by themselves, they'll die!). Their number one goal in life is to have fun.

They're optimistic, visionary, dynamic, enthusiastic and persuasive.

Expressives are demonstrative in both words and language.

They're generally good starters but can be poor finishers as they get easily bored and distracted.

Expressives as entrepreneurs do well in marketing, advertising, arts and sales.

The best way to work with an Expressive is to be stimulating.

How to influence an Expressive:

- Focus on the future and possibilities.
- Stay "big picture" focused.
- Present yourself and information enthusiastically.
- Be creative.
- Offer new ideas.
- Show flexibility with deadlines.
- Give them attention.
- Be friendly and sociable.
- Mirror words and use words and phrases such as 'enjoyment', 'talk to people'.

Avoid tying them down to routine or boring them with details.

Amiables

For an Amiable, people's welfare and relationships always come first. Friendships are very important to an Amiable.

Amiables work with and through people to achieve outcomes. They're the peacemakers, nurturers, and rescuers. They are also sharing, caring, supporting, patient and loyal.

They don't like conflict and avoid it at all costs. They want to see everyone live and work in harmony.

They tend to be the most stressed of the four personality styles as they want to put others first before themselves, and find it very hard to say no.

Amiables often become social workers, teachers, doctors, nurses, and administrators.

The best way to work with an Amiable is to be agreeable.

How to influence an Amiable:

- Focus on them as a person (take time to schmooze) – check emotions.
- Be interested in them – find areas of common interest.
- Ask "how" questions to encourage them to contribute an opinion and give them time to answer.
- Be informal, sincere and open.
- Provide support.
- Praise their efforts.
- Listen more, listen better.
- Show how ideas will impact people.
- Be patient and supportive.
- Slow down and work at their pace.

Avoid taking advantage of their good nature or springing last minute surprises on them.

Analyticals

Analyticals love systems and don't you dare mess with the system! They love documentation that tells them how to do their job – policies/procedures, manuals, job descriptions, and instruction books. Quality is hugely important; they're perfectionists – I's have to be dotted and T's need to be crossed.

Analyticals love data. They need data – lots of it – to make a decision. Don't rush them in their decision making; give them plenty of time. They ask questions, are quite formal in their approach and are generally cautious.

They tend to be engineers, surveyors, accountants, lawyers, pilots, and surgeons.

The best way to work with an Analytical is to be accurate.

How to influence an Analytical:

- Complete all preparation work in advance.
- Be thorough - back up all facts and figures and provide practical examples.
- Provide both sides to an argument.
- Take your time and give them time to consider proposals.
- Present timetables.
- Give space, silence and support.
- Communicate in writing.

Avoid being overly emotional or casual with important issues, don't keep changing things without good justification or vaguely answer questions.

In addition to the above, you might find the following helpful:

Analyticals and Drivers tend to be work oriented and make decisions based on logic.

Expressives and Amiables tend to be relationship oriented and make decisions based on emotion.

Analyticals and Amiables listen more and are less assertive.

Expressives and Drivers talk more and are more assertive.

Robyn found having an understanding of personality styles helpful when she was dealing with clients. She was able to pick up very quickly within a few minutes of meeting someone what their personality style was and she adapted her discussions to this, e.g. one person she met for the first time talked really fast and was all about work. He was a Driver. Robyn focused on work, matched this person's rate of speech and didn't waste time. In another instance, the person wanted to talk about the weather, life in general, family and friends and time was not an issue. This person was an Amiable. Robyn conversed with this person for a while before she led the discussion around to work. In both instances Robyn was successful in securing training work. She was able to build immediate rapport with these people quickly and adapt to their style.

How to Use Personality Groups

If you are employing people you need to have a balance of personalities in your business. Too many Expressives and life is one big party. Too many Drivers and it's the classic case of too many cooks and not enough Indians.

We tend to gravitate to people who are similar to us because we can relate to them. We can find it difficult to work with people who have a different personality to us; differences can cause conflict if people don't recognize or adapt to each other's style or work preference. However, we also work well with people who are completely opposite to us because our different strengths make up a whole.

Once you understand someone's approach and preferences, working together becomes less about differences and more about taking advantage of complementary strengths.

Note: We label jars not people so it's important not to pigeon-hole people. Also, most of us can operate in more than one personality style, depending on the situation.

Summary

We tend to operate predominantly under one personality. Knowing what your personality style is will help you to work with others. Once you understand someone's approach and preferences, working together becomes less about differences and more about taking advantage of complementary strengths.

Exercise

1   Identify what your dominant personality is. How might you need to change the way you work or communicate with other personality styles?

2   Write down the different types of personalities you might need in your team. Is there a balance?

Notes

Chapter 20 – Women and Men in Business

This is another chapter that's difficult to write. For many of you, it may also be difficult to read but it contains a lot of things that need to be said and perhaps, more importantly, understood by both sexes.

Originally we'd planned on two chapters; one on women in business and one on men in business. However, when Bob received Robyn's draft on women in business he quickly realized she had done an excellent job of reflecting the differences between men and women and how much of what she'd written actually applied to both.

One final note. A lot of what we say in this chapter are in fact generalizations. That, however, does not make them any less true or valuable. So, as with everything else in our book, do as you will with what we say. It's provided to make you aware and make you think. And all of us don't think alike.

Without further ado, Bob will borrow muchly (a kiwi word for a *lot*) from Robyn's draft attempt to sound as smart as she is, and write the introduction.

Bob's Introduction

While both men and women can be successful in running a business, they each have different strengths, and weaknesses. Their strengths can often complement each other and their weaknesses offset one another, but as you'll see in both this introduction and Robyn's observations, they can clash too.

A little soap box speech first. Even though the Women's Rights Movement has been fighting for women's equality since the world's first women's rights convention in1848, there is still an inherited predisposition or belief that women are inferior to men. This belief still exists, even among the most educated men in business today.

For Bob, the realization that women are not only built differently than men, they are wired differently too, came early in life. Compared to men, he found women:

- Tend to lead a much more balanced life.
- Observe, absorb and process more information before reaching a conclusion.
- Are more emotional and therefore recognize its effect and impact on things.

Bob also noticed that while these traits can be used to complement men's thinking and help provide a much more rounded picture of things, women were (and still are) often criticized for these traits.

"If you were more dedicated to your job, you'd be coming in on weekends like I do."

"Stop looking at every nit-picky detail and just make a decision!"

"You're way too emotional. We need to leave emotion out of this!

As you'll see in Robyn's observations, she learned the same things, by being on the receiving end of many comments like those above.

Okay, so what's the point of all this? Well, let's start with a few facts Robyn dug up.

According to Charlotte Bunch, a distinguished professor in the Department of Women's and Gender Studies at Rutgers, *the state of the world today demands that women become less modest and dream/plan/act/risk on a larger scale.*

Women have obviously gotten that message because the numbers of women owning and managing their own businesses has been steadily increasing.

From 2013-2016 the number of women who set up their own business rose by 45 percent, compared to just 27 percent among men, a team at Aston University, United Kingdom discovered.

It is estimated that in 2016 there were just over 11.3 million women-owned businesses in the United States, employing nearly 9 million people and generating over $1.6 trillion in revenues (Source: The State of Women Owned Businesses).

In New Zealand in 2006, 36 percent of women were self-employed (Source: Statistics New Zealand, 2203; 2007).

All of that means that, more than ever, men and women need to work together to help each other become more successful; to share their strong points and help each other work through their weak points.

I think you'll find Robyn's observations and suggested ways in which men and women can share their different views, strengths, experiences and support each other extremely helpful.

Robyn's Observations

Gender Mix and Management Styles

When I was a personal assistant, I worked in a small not-for-profit organisation which provided leadership and growth opportunities for girls and young women. It made sense that because it was an organisation whose customers were girls and young women that the staff would also be predominantly women.

Previous to this I had worked in a small department where I was the only female, as well as organizations with a balance of men and women. So my experience spans working with mainly men, mainly women and gender balanced organizations.

Needless to say I learnt a lot about working with both genders, about how men and women think differently and after working at the not-for-profit organisation I learnt that for an organisation to be fully functional there should be a mix of both genders to offer balanced opinions and ideas.

The main differences between men and women I noted were:

- When presenting, a man with an issue would immediately go into problem solving mode – the logical and the practical. This was great, but quite often they missed the emotional part of the situation. I needed to tell them what people were feeling about something and why.

- Women can be too emotional. Yes, we cry because we're a sensitive bunch and we care about people. I have never seen a man cry in the workplace.

- If a man has an issue with what you did or what you said they will tell you directly. Women tend to talk about other people behind their backs and gossip instead of dealing with the person or situation.

- Men tend to be more arrogant.

- Women are more likely to be less confident and less likely to admit it.

- Women tend to make decisions based on instinct. They can't explain the decision they've made other than it felt right or it didn't feel right.

- The goal of men in meetings is often to be the alpha male and gain territory. Women's main aim in meetings is to build relationships.

I would never again work in an organization that was too loaded towards one gender. There needs to be a balance when you're working on an issue that needs to be looked at from both practical, logical and emotional viewpoints.

So this is important to consider when you're hiring staff.

Often I have been asked who makes better managers, men or women? This was a question that I wondered about for many years. I thought about the strengths and weaknesses of the men and women I had worked with and I found it hard to actually come up with an answer until I realized that it wasn't so much about management or leadership styles, it was more to do with personalities. It was the personality of that individual rather than whether they were male or female that made them successful in business, the way they treated staff and the way staff viewed them. We touched on personality styles in Chapter 19 and we'll touch more on leadership skills in Chapter 25.

***

Some other tips that I learned that might be helpful to both men and women:

Mentoring

As I embarked on my new self-employment venture I decided I needed a couple of mentors.

I chose two.

One was a woman I'll call Sydney. I admired her because she'd had a difficult past, had started her own business and grew.

The other was a man I'll call Cameron, who I'd met through a networking group. Cameron was down-to-earth and ran a landscaping business and was always willing to help and provide me with advice. Cameron taught me three things: To value myself and the work that I do and therefore my charge-out rates should reflect that, and to learn to ask for what I wanted.

Over a period of 18 months, I'd meet up with Sydney or Cameron over coffee and they were great sounding boards, just to help when I needed to know what direction to take, when I needed a second opinion or when I was about to give up.

So what does a mentor do and how do you find one?

The Merriam-Webster WWWebster Dictionary defines a mentor as a "trusted counselor or guide". Mentor comes from the Greek word meaning enduring.

Mentoring is an informal relationship and involves sharing, learning, seeking assistance and is mentee driven.

The original Mentor is a character in Homer's poem *The Odyssey*. When Odysseus, King of Ithaca, went to fight in the Trojan War, he entrusted the care of his kingdom to Mentor. Mentor served as the teacher and overseer of Odysseys' son, Telemachus.

A mentor will generally guide and teach using their own experience as a base. Often a mentor will also share challenges and obstacles they have had to overcome in their own journey.

How to find a mentor

1. Write down some names of people who you admire (these could be people you know or be famous people). Think about people in your workplace, in the community, who you play sports with or socialize with. Could any of these people be your mentor?

   (Hint: think about picking a mentor, at least one, of the opposite sex.)

2. Why do you admire these people? The following is a list of qualities that may help:

   Honesty
   Vision oriented
   Inspirational
   Competent
   Good communicator
   Dependable
   Trustworthy
   Consistent
   Confident
   Fair
   Open to ideas
   Motivator
   Assertive
   Recognises good performance
   Goal oriented
   Change promoter
   Good at managing their time
   Interpersonal
   Multi tasker
   Seeks knowledge
   (Adapted from: Team Power by Jim Temme)

When you meet with your mentor establish some guidelines. How can the mentor help you? How often will you meet? What will you do, if anything, after each meeting?

Ask For Help

Women quite often feel they have to do everything because we quite often do do everything! But sometimes we need to swallow our pride, recognize when things aren't working or that we do need help. We can never know it all. We don't have all of the skills needed to run a business and it's OK to ask for help.

When I first started in business I tried to do everything mainly to save money, but I also wanted to learn how to do things. After a while I realized I was running myself into the ground, working longer and longer hours and spending a lot of time trying to work out stuff where I just didn't have the skill or knowledge. My business was tipping my life balance scale way out of balance!

Now, I have no problems asking for help and if that means I have to pay for it, then so be it. In the end it saves me time; I keep someone else in business and a chance for that person to use their skills.

Network and Learn, Learn, Learn

In 2004 the Organisation for Economic Co-operation and Development (OECD) identified social networks as one of the more important factors in business success.

Networking is a key component of being successful in business, and women are very good at this. I have been a member of a number of women-only groups where meeting topics have revolved around the specific challenges women in business face. There is certainly a need for these types of groups. The New Zealand Women's

Entrepreneur Network which was established in 2017, only took a few months to achieve a membership of 2,200.

It is so important to keep up-to-date with what is happening in your industry and the business world, locally and globally. Not only does networking help you connect with people but you might also get some work.

Read magazines, do Internet research, join online social media groups. You are only as good as the last job you did for your client. To keep the competitive edge you must continue to learn or else you'll get left behind and your techniques and thinking will become outdated.

While running a business I attended and presented at numerous personal assistant conferences and joined various business networking groups. At these courses and meetings I learned about current trends, how to improve what I was doing and how to share my knowledge and experiences with others.

Working From Home

There are many advantages of running a business from home mainly convenience and cost savings. But there can be disadvantages too.

These are my tips for working from home:

1   *Have a dedicated work space*

When I first established my secretarial business I set up a small desk in a corner of a room in my house. After a while, however, work ended up in the bedroom, the lounge and on the dining room table. Not only did this get untidy it also prevented me from mentally switching off from work. Every time I saw the paperwork, I was tempted to pick it up and work on it, even if it was outside of work hours.

2   *Close/lock the office door*

It can become too convenient popping into the office to look at something at 11 on Sunday morning as this-can quickly become 2 on Sunday afternoon. I now shut the office door on weekends so I'm not tempted to work.

3   *Office phone line*

For the first three years of my secretarial business, my home phone line was also my office phone, which meant the phone had to be answered at all times in a professional manner. The answer-phone message was quite long too because it contained instructions for leaving messages for both my personal and business life. Once again, there was no clear separation of home and work so in my fourth year of business I decided to get a dedicated business line, which meant when the business phone rang after 5 pm I could choose not to answer it.

4   *Business is business*

Be clear to your friends and family that even though you are working from home, it is not a good time for them to drop in or ring for a chat.

Work/Life Balance

Yeah, we've all experienced the achingly long days and weeks where we've done nothing but work, work, work! It's easy to get on that roundabout but oh so difficult to get off it.

If you're an established business, work is always going to be there. If you're just starting out it's hard not to let the pursuit of a dollar take over or because we love what we do so much it doesn't feel like work so we're always working.

But we can't keep working long hours day after day and it's important to take time out.

Here are my tips for work/life balance:

1   Schedule your day so that you work between specific times only e.g. 8.00 am to 4.30 pm. When 4.30 pm comes around, it's no more work! It's now your time. Make an appointment with yourself to do things such as go to the gym, go to the hairdresser, watch the kids play soccer. Guard that time with your life!

2   Resist the temptation to check emails or social media accounts outside of work hours. I know that we need to be flexible but most of us don't need to be connected to our businesses 24/7. Most of us have got caught up in the FOMO (Fear of Missing Out) trap when we should be in JOMO (Joy of Missing Out) mode.

3   Take regular breaks throughout the day. Remember to eat. We don't expect our car to keep going unless it is topped up with fuel. The same goes for us; we need to eat regularly and we need to take the time for a breather. Go for a quick walk around the block to get some fresh air and exercise.

What Robyn Learned

As a woman, this is what I have learnt about being in business:

- Ask for help! You can't do everything.

- Pursue every opportunity.

- Be nice to everyone (Especially Bob!). You never know when someone may become a client.

- Be thoroughly organized.

- Learn how to cope with stress.

- I did it! I am living my passion, living my dream.

- It's not the destination that matters – it's the journey made along the way.

What advice would I give to both men and women who are thinking about going into business?

Dream

Dream big dreams and have patience as they unfold.

Get Serious

Be focused – have a plan with objectives and strategies clearly defined. Find a mentor who can help you achieve your goals.

Commit

Put it in writing. Tell people. Believe in yourself, your purpose, your destiny.

Learn

Keep learning and reading and be open to new ideas and opportunities.

Surround yourself with Positive People

Are your friends encouraging and supportive or do they drain your energy with their negativity? Don't let others sabotage your dreams or desires.

Courage

Be brave – step outside your comfort zone.

Persistence

Never give up – never give in.

Do it now!

Take responsibility for your life. Don't wait. Your life isn't going to. Life's clock ticks on relentlessly.

Stop thinking and talking about your dream – take action. Go do it! Now!

Yay! Robyn's asked me to throw in some of my advice too.

The first one is actually hers.

Don't be a political ladder climber!

Continue to learn, stretch yourself, and use your skills and knowledge to build your business and dreams on a sound base.

Treat people the way you want to be treated!

Be patient, kind and understanding. Think, don't react. Use your senses to read people. Help them learn and grow and you'll find you'll grow with them.

For women and men

Be proud, confident and, most of all, believe in yourself. Treat each other as equals, learn from each other, support each other. The minute you think you're superior is the minute you've started down the road to failure.

Treat your business as a business

- Don't try to be everything to everybody. Be a lot good at a little, not a little good at a lot.

- Don't let your dream become a nightmare. Learn all you can before you commit to a business.

- If you want to drink and socialize with your buddies or girlfriends, do it at home. Don't turn your business into a man cave, women's social club, friend's hangout or family reunion hall.

- Don't open a restaurant just because you like to cook. Eating and socializing are also not critical business skills.

- Make sure you know how much money you'll need and where it's going to come from. (Don't forget a backup stash to pay off Guido and a vacation pamphlet in case things don't go as planned.)

- Always, always, always, have a plan B and plan C. A plan A would be good here too!

Summary and Exercise
No matter what, keep your sense of humor, stay happy and healthy and have fun.

***

OH NO! NOT ANOTHER AUTHORS' NOTE!

Yes, we know this chapter has kind of turned into a free for all for us. But the chapter is near and dear to both of our hearts and, as you've learned, we've a lot to say about a lot.

Oh, and it's our book so, we can do what we want.

Neener neener neener.

Notes

Chapter 21 – Employees

Now that we've covered the various personality types, and the differences between women and men, let's take a look at some of the people you'll likely bring into your business life.

This chapter will be short but nonetheless extremely important. If your business is big enough that you'll hire employees to help you run it, then you'll do well to pay attention to some of the things we suggest in this chapter.

A few facts we tend to forget about employees:

- They're the face of your business.
- Often they're the ones running it.
- In many ways, they're responsible for your businesse's success or failure, and
- Finally, you're responsible for them.

Skill Needs

Before you start dealing with who to hire, take a few moments to assess the needs of your business.

Start by listing the tasks you plan to do. Then ask yourself, do you have the knowledge and skills to do each task? Will you have time to do all of it? The tendency here will be to overload yourself so once you have your list, take a step back and reassess it. Can you honestly do all of it, and do it accurately?

Remember, trying to do more than you really know you can or winging the things you don't know enough about, will quickly get your business in trouble. So, be honest. If you can't do something, for whatever reason, move it to the following list so you can find an acceptable way to get it done.

Next, what types of skills will someone need to do the tasks you can't get to or are not qualified to do?

Finally, try to group the tasks and skills that seem to go together; skill sets that a single person would need to do multiple tasks.

What you should be left with is a rough idea of how many people you'll need to run your business.

Yeah, we know. You're already trying to reduce the number of employees by assigning stuff to people you don't think will be very busy with what you've given them. But hang in there with us for a few minutes so we can help you do that logically.

Who to Hire

Let's take a look at the time you think each task will take. Also, is it something that needs to be done multiple times; daily, weekly or monthly? e.g. a cook or waitress would need to prepare or serve several meals, say every five to ten minutes during each day. But someone would only need to balance the books once a week or monthly.

Once you're done, sort out the occasional jobs then try to combine as many of the remaining tasks as makes sense considering the skills, time required and don't forget, common sense, e.g. the cook or waitress may have down time, but you'll not likely want them cleaning the restrooms between making or serving meals. Likewise, we doubt many accountants would be willing to clean restrooms but, what about the dishwasher?

For the occasional jobs, and those that require special skills, you'll probably want to contract those out.

In the end, you should have a fairly good idea of what size staff you'll likely need and what skills they should have.

Personality Traits

Next to each job or task, list the personality traits that you think are important for the person you hire or assign it to. Remember, for front of the house employees, those with direct customer contact, they are the face of your business.

However, don't ignore the back of the house employees. The last thing you want is your cook throwing a plateful of food through the serving window because a customer didn't like it. Or a writer in your writer support business telling a customer to get lost because their head is in the story they're writing.

Once you think you have a complete list of jobs, sorted by skills and personality traits, it's time to move on to the hiring process

The above approach may seem a bit childish or rote but remember, it's our job to make you think. By suggesting you lay out the tasks based on time, skill and personality requirements we think that will force you to dig deep into what you'll need to make your business a success and keep things running smoothly. We also hope this approach will give you a much better appreciation for each person you hire and the role they'll play in your business.

Then too, nothing says you need to use this approach, or any other. So feel free to use your own approach or skip this step totally and just wing it, which is what a lot of small business owners do. Either way, we've already got you thinking and accomplished our goal.

Interviews and Salary Offers

By now you should be armed with enough information to begin interviewing potential employees.

Remember, no matter what their position, they run your business and are, to some degree, responsible for its success or failure. Thus, make sure they have or can develop the skills your business will need. Also, make sure their personality fits too. There is nothing worse than an always serious person trying to sell your humorous children's stories. (See Chapter 19 Personalities.)

Interviews

Many people just starting a new business have never interviewed people before. So, following are some suggestions and common interview questions to help make the interview comfortable for both parties.

Because your business may not exist yet or, if it does, the potential employee may have no way to investigate it, think about beginning the interview with:

- A description of your business.
- What your products and/or services are.
- Where it will be located, if you're not conducting the interview there.
- How you expect it to grow.

Next, give them a very brief description of the job they're applying for. Tell them what you expect from them in their day to day tasks, their interplay with other employees, opportunities you'll provide and any other expectations or benefits of the job.

Common Interview Questions

The following are some common interview questions you might ask: (We would suggest that you tell them there are no right or wrong answers and wanting to learn new things and move up to a better position is good.)

- Tell me (us) about yourself and why you think you might be a good fit for the position we're offering?
- How do you see your experience fitting in with our needs?
- How fast do you think you could come up to speed and why?
- Do you see this as a long-term position or a stepping stone to something better or different?
- How do your strengths fit with our position and how would you deal with things that are not part of your strong suit?

Finally, don't be afraid to open with or insert questions to help break the ice or provide the interviewee with an easy way to show how they can contribute.

- Any other talents that are not on your resume? Like being a member of a band we could hire for our grand opening or having a granny that knits mittens we could purchase for giveaways?
- Before we get started (or into the next part), I (we) love to read. Any suggestions on good books you've read lately?
-

Benefits

One last thing. Anyone you interview is likely to ask questions about what benefits come with the job. So, be sure you've decided on what insurance benefits (medical, dental, life, etc.) you'll provide. The number of vacation and sick days they can take and how they'll be paid for each, your rules for overtime and how they'll be paid for extra hours.

Finally, don't forget about employee discounts on products you sell or services you provide and opportunities for them to invest in your business.

Salary Offers

As for salary offers, would you turn over your business being successful or not to someone making $12 an hour? We wouldn't.

Make sure each of your offers is competitive and fairly compensate the person for their skills. Remember, they're the face of your business.

Finally, don't forget, you're responsible for them!

- They're your business family so treat them like family.
- Help them obtain new skills, new schooling.
- Provide them with medical and dental coverage if you can; if not for their whole family, then at least for them. (See Insurance, Chapter 15).
- Pay them overtime when you've asked them to stay beyond their normal hours or they fill in for someone who didn't show up.

Volunteers, Interns and Mentees

If you're in a position to have volunteers or interns in your company, we suggest you treat them just as you would any other employee. Remember, volunteers have given up their time to help your business be successful.

People in these positions have typically taken them to be mentored so they can gain experience they're lacking or to learn something new. Often, however, they're looked upon as unequal to other employees. But they're not. They're just trying to fill a hole in their experience and they've placed their faith in you to help them.

We think too that you'll find them much more eager to learn, to question things that don't make sense and to offer to help with even the simplest of tasks as long as they're still learning.

Hire a Veteran

Bob once had someone respond with, "Why would I want to hire someone whose only experience is carrying the base plate to a mortar?" when he suggested the person think about hiring a veteran to fill a position he had open.

Even though Bob knew the guy was kidding, Bob lit into him. "Aside from obviously being smarter than you, a veteran, no matter what his job in the service was, will have skills any business can use."

Had Bob over reacted? He doesn't think so. You see he went into the Air Force as a high school dropout and came out:

- With a high school diploma.
- Having completed all of his freshmen college classes.
- Having completed three technical and two management schools.
- With three years of experience in maintenance of ground and aircraft systems.
- With two years of management experience.

Wow! All of that in only thirty years! (Actually, it was six. That's six not sixty.)

More important, like many others, he had matured (Stop laughing Robyn!), learned the value of teamwork, worked with a wide variety of personalities and been exposed to many different jobs ranging from simple to extremely complex.

Perhaps the most important thing he learned was to appreciate and learn from the differences in people. The fact that we don't all think alike, react alike or see things the same.

Is he unique? No.
(Robyn here: He actually is unique, but don't tell him that. His head's big enough as it is!)

Talk to anyone who has spent time in the military and you'll find they are much more mature and have a better understanding of life in general, the good and the bad. They understand how to be a leader as well as take directions. You'll also find they are dedicated to not only completing what they're assigned but also helping others and working in a team environment.

Summary

In this chapter we've tried to cover employees, the role they play and how to choose them.

We've also given you one approach to determining the skills your business will need, how many employees you'll need to fill those skill sets and the personalities that would best reflect your business. Then we added some hints and examples to use when interviewing and establishing benefits and salary offers.

Finally, we reminded you of your responsibilities as an employer and/or as a mentor.

Exercise

As we did in the chapter, make a list of the skills your business will need and try and arrange them into task-oriented jobs. Now divide them into part-time and full-time jobs.

Next to each job, list the personality traits and skills you'll look for in applicants.

For the part-time jobs, decide if you want to hire someone to do them or contract them out.

For the part-time and full-time positions you envision creating, research like businesses for similar positions and assign a job title, create a job description and a competitive salary range for each.

Then for each position, create a list of interview questions that you can refer to during the interview. Remember, even if the position is part time or you're contracting it out, you still need to interview the person to make sure they're qualified and will fit in with your business style.

Finally, identify any positions where you think hiring a veteran, an intern or having someone volunteer to fill the position may provide an opportunity for you to pay it forward by helping someone worthy of being helped.

Finally, list the benefits and rules that apply in general or vary by job.

You're now ready to start advertising and interviewing!

Notes

Chapter 22 – Family, Friends and Strangers

Do's and Don'ts

This chapter will touch on some very emotional stuff. Some of you may not like the messages we give you. Others may think it doesn't apply to them, their family or friends.

However, we strongly advise that you read what we have to say. Why? Because we've seen countless business owners lose family and friends because they too didn't think it applied to them.

Remember what we said in the beginning about stress? Well, this is where the stress of starting, running and dealing with your everyday business issues can easily drive a wedge into those wonderful, close ties you have with your family and friends.

Family and Friends

Some Do's First

Do involve your family and friends in your business. They don't have to help you run it but, like it or not, when you come home in a nasty mood they'll be the ones who have to deal with you.

Do discuss things with them and ask their opinions.

Do let them help in solving problems, addressing issues or just be a sounding board when you need to hear yourself talk.

The Don'ts

We can't emphasize this next bit of advice enough.

Don't borrow money from friends or family unless you absolutely have no other choice! Or if you no longer want anything to do with them.

Don't borrow equipment or items for your business from friends or family.

Accepting donations is fine, but make sure everyone agrees they are donations! If you do borrow from friends or family, be prepared to deal with losing their friendship or causing major strife in your family life if your business hits a rocky road or fails.

If they've invested in your business treat it as you would any other loan. Work out a payment schedule and stick to it. As uncomfortable as it may be, discuss what will happen if you can't make payments or default entirely.

Likewise, if you borrow equipment ensure you intend to return it or replace if it is worn beyond use. Again, have the agreement in writing so that there are no misunderstandings.

Just because they're family doesn't mean you can forget about paying them or returning items when things don't go right. Nor does it mean they're going to drop everything and jump in and bail your ass out of trouble! This is your dream, not theirs!

Don't hire your friends or relatives unless you really have to. Like borrowing from them, it typically causes a bunch of problems you don't need. If you do, make sure they clearly understand what's expected of them and treat them as you would any other employee, especially if you have other employees.

An additional word of caution. Friends and family members often think they can do things other employees wouldn't dare do simply because they're related or know you. For example, "borrowing" supplies, taking money from the till, taking "free samples" or giving them to friends or customers, coming in late or not showing up at all. All reasons why you really don't want to go there!

On the flip side, don't expect your friends and family to work for free or jump in and bail you out, unless they are partners in your business. This is your dream and your obligation, not theirs (We can't say that enough!). If they offer or you ask them to help, make sure you clearly define what it is you want or need them to do and what you expect of them. And, if at all possible, pay them as you would any other employee.

Strangers

Do ask opinions of other merchants, customers and anyone willing to give you a minute. Run ideas by them. Ask their advice, what would they do, what have they done that worked or didn't work?

When Bob had his restaurant, the lunch crowd was primarily people who owned businesses or worked in the nearby area. When they were developing their lunch menu they went from store to store in town and asked the people who worked there what kind of sandwiches and other items they would like to see on the lunch menu. Not to brag, but they did one of the best lunch businesses in town!

Do ask your family, friends and nearby business owners for their support. Ask them to come by and take a tour, eat there, drink there, buy their produce there, avail themselves of whatever product you sell or service you provide and render an opinion. If they like what they see, ask them to spread the word, hand out your business cards, tweet their friends, like you on Facebook or rate you on Yelp. If they don't like what they see ask them to be honest and tell you why, what you can do better or how to fix the problem.

We know, we know. Many of you are saying, "Sure, like I'm really going to just go ask some stranger on the street 'Hey, you there! Taste this! So, whatta ya think about my meatballs?'"

Our answer to that is to do what you are comfortable with. If you're okay with doing it, why not try standing in front of your restaurant and asking people to try some of your food. We think you'll be surprised at how many people will gladly stop, try it and give you their opinion. Not only will most of them be happy you asked, but in all likelihood they'll come back to try out your restaurant if they like what they tasted.

Note: If you run a funeral home we wouldn't advise standing out front and asking people to try out your coffins unless, of course, your business is in a neighborhood frequented by vampires. If it is, our congratulations on an excellent location choice!

One final thought. For other business owners, don't forget to return the favor! Do support the "other guy" by doing the same for them. Is there a business down the street where you get your copies made, have lunch, or stop in for a drink after work? Be sure and refer your customers to them. Keep some of their business cards in a holder on your counter. Whatever works!

Whenever we receive great service we're not bashful about telling other people. Bob also carries two-three business cards from his friend's wine bar in his wallet and never misses an opportunity to recommend them. Why? Because they offer a great selection of wines and beers, and outstanding service! Plus he's been where they are and understands how every little bit helps!

Summary

Involving family and friends in your business can be fun, but it can also have some serious consequences. Likewise, don't be afraid to involve strangers. Ask for their opinions, advice and their support.

Finally, don't forget that support works both ways.

Exercise

Make a list of things in your business that you think family or friends might be able to help with.

Also, compile a list of what questions to ask family, friends and strangers, e.g.

- Is our service excellent or just okay?
- What products should we add? etc

Notes

Chapter 23 – Partners

This will be another very short but extremely important subject. Which is why we left it as a chapter.

Dealing with partners is very much like dealing with family, friends and strangers. In many cases they will likely be family or friends.

But partners more than likely will have a much bigger impact on not only your business but your personal life and/or your relationship with them.

If you have or plan to take on one or more partners, there are some things you should resolve right up front.

Partnership Agreement

Clearly define the role of each partner. This is extremely important, and it needs to be in writing, typically in the form of a partnership agreement.

The agreement should define:

- Percentage of ownership for each partner.
- Who does what?
- Responsibilities, what is each partner in charge of?
- How much authority do they have in each area?
- Areas where they have no say.
- If things are to be decided by vote, are all votes equal?
- Silent partner? How silent?

Rules for partners:

- Can they come on site to your business and direct employees?
- Can they represent the business to customers and, if so, to what extent?
- Can they remove cash from the till, order things to eat for free, use business supplies and equipment for their personal use?
- In case of conflict, how are things to be resolved?

Also, how things are to be divided up or liquidated if the business should (heaven forbid) fail, or be sold, as well as, who will be responsible for dissolving or transferring your business:

- Notification submittals to state, local the other government agencies.
- Cancelation or transfer of permits, licenses, and ficticious business names.
- Payment of taxes and debts, and from where?
- Notification to creditors, employees, and customers.
- Division and distribution of remaining profits, if any.
- If applicable, division of business assets, or
- Equipment and asset liquidation and how they're to be liquidated.

Summary

For businesses with partners, we've tried to identify some of the things that should be defined in a partnership agreement.

Exercise

If you have or are planning on having partners in your business, draft up a partnership agreement. Cover as much of the above information as possible and anything else you think should be in there.

Remember, it's a lot easier to cross things out as you finalize your agreement then it is to discover years later that you left out something critical.

Once you're finished, we strongly suggest you have an attorney look over it to make sure it covers everything.

Notes

Chapter 24 – Management and Leadership Skills

Management and leadership are often confused. The simplest way to distinguish between them is to remember: You manage things, and lead people.

Yes, we know. We often talk about managing people, but in reality we're not managing them; we're managing the tasks we want them to perform. We're directing them to perform a specific task, sequence of tasks, or interface with one another to accomplish something.

That direction often dictates that they follow an approved system, set of rules or controls and the manager measures their performance or output using approved standards to determine if they are doing things right and are successful.

Another way to think of management is to see it as directing action down a predetermined path to hopefully assure its successful completion.

Both management and leadership skills are important to how successful your business will be and how employees perceive you.

Most business owners believe they can manage pretty well. While we don't quite agree with that, we will concede that management skills can be learned or training in this area can enhance whatever skills an owner might already have. Certainly, someone with management skills and experience in your business field can be hired.

And what about leaders? There is a lot of debate as to whether people are born leaders or if leadership can be taught. Robyn believes it's a bit of both. Bob believes it's both but heavily swayed toward born leadership qualities.

There are certainly some natural born leaders, e.g. Nelson Mandela, Bono from U2, Ritchie McCaw (ex All Blacks captain), but most of us have to work hard to lead and constantly remind ourselves to lead and not manage.

So what's the difference?

Leaders are innovative, they develop things, and they rely on their trust in people to do things right. They lead people by example and by nurturing them, rather than telling them what to do and how to do it.

Do all people want to be led and not managed? No. Of course not. It often depends heavily on the situation.

For example, a young student who works at a hamburger place flipping burgers to earn money while going to school, may not care about being led, nurtured or innovative. That is, unless they're interested in eventually opening their own hamburger place someday. Even there though, they're probably more interested in business operations then flipping burgers.

This too is typical of people with and without inherent leadership skills. If they're just there to earn money and don't think there's anything to be learned, they likely don't have good leadership skills. But if they pay attention to other aspects of the business, what's selling because they're making more of that than other things or start to teach others the proper way to flip burgers, they very likely have inherent leadership skills.

Put another way, people with good leadership skills see opportunity in almost everything they do. Opportunity to learn new things, to grow and to apply something in some way to their lives.

Most successful businesses require both skills – you'll need to manage and to lead.

Think back to some of our comments in the very front of this book where we told you drinking with your buddies or being able to cook are not skills critical to the success of your business. However, assigning and managing the tasks performed by your employees are. Likewise, involving them in other areas of the business to keep them interested and help them grow is something you'll find you need to do if you want to retain the really valuable employees.

Robyn has an excellent example of where she had to hone and use her leadership skills:

I'd always been interested in emergency management, how people and communities coped, supported each other and worked together during a natural disaster.

I decided to volunteer for Civil Defence, the organization responsible for rescuing people, co-ordination resources and other emergency management services and looking after the welfare of people during a natural disaster.

I joined the New Brighton Sector Post as a welfare officer. New Brighton was a beach suburb that looked out over the Pacific Ocean. It was a community that would have to deal with a variety of different potential disasters – earthquakes, tsunami, snow (like the big snow that crippled Christchurch in 1992), major wind storms and flooding from the Avon River. One of the biggest concerns was that in a major earthquake, one or both of the two bridges leading into and out of New Brighton would collapse, reducing or eliminating access.

During our monthly meetings we took part in mock regional disaster exercises and learnt how to process evacuees, and their pets, as they arrived at the sector post if they were displaced from their homes.

But training wasn't just about disasters and processing people. It was also about developing leadership skills: communicating under stress, team building, problem solving and good decision-making.

Below is a summary of one of the workshops I attended about problem solving.

We were given an exercise to do in a group which was called the Zin Obelisk Challenge. We were to pretend that we were part of an archaeological team and had discovered the burial site of Queen Nephrodite in a pyramid in the city of Memphis.

Beside the tomb of Queen Nephrodite stood a solid, rectangular obelisk, called a zin, which was built in her honour. The structure took less than two weeks to complete. The team's task was to determine on which day of the week the obelisk was completed and we only had 25 minutes to complete the task. We were each given pieces of information related to the task. We were allowed to share this information orally but weren't allowed to show it to other team members. If we got the correct answer within the time limit we had worked together successfully as a team.

I was nominated leader.

As we got closer and closer to the strict time limit of 25 minutes, it was unclear to me what was the right answer.

We got down to one minute.

Two answers were being debated.

Tick, tick...

Thirty seconds.

Arguments were strong for both answers.

Tick, tick.

Fifteen seconds.

The answer was becoming clearer.

Ten seconds.

The facilitator asked me, "What's the answer?"

I looked at her in panic. I had an idea, but wasn't sure.

Tick, tick.

"Robyn, time's up. What's the answer?"

My heart thudded so loudly I thought I personally could create a natural disaster.

"Um..."

"Robyn."

"The sixth working day."

"That answer is... correct."

I let out a huge sigh of relief.

The exercise had a number of key learning points about leadership:

- The leader needed to ensure everyone fully participated. Someone could've had a vital piece of information that they hadn't given or been encouraged to give or wasn't being listened to.

- Maintaining effective communication is critical when a team is at work (and under stress)

- Recognizing that members have different skills and aptitudes; it is important to fully tap them.

- Recognizing that members are comfortable with different roles in the team.

This exercise taught me that making a decision is important and with the additional pressure of a time limit, all critical skills of the team need to be recognized so team members can be organized and pointed to where their skills best served reaching the team's goal.

At the end of the exercise I quickly realized how these skills could also be transferred back into my business: To use them to direct those working for me or hired to do a task to be organized to work as a team.

Summary

This chapter defined the differences between managing things and leading people to accomplish things related to your business.

Exercise

Think about what areas of your business you may need to develop and apply management or leadership skills to.

List your goals for each area and the steps needed to achieve them. Then divide the steps for each goal into things you can direct (manage) to get done and things you can inspire (lead) people to do on their own.

Finally, for each task, list your criteria for determining that the task was completed successfully.

Notes

Chapter 25 - Time Management

Good time management skills are critical to be able to run a business well.

The standard tips around having a to do list and keeping a diary, whether that be paper based or electronic, is important. However, time management can go a lot deeper than that.

When Robyn was running both her secretarial and training business it wasn't unusual for her to be working twelve-hour days. She ran around like a mad thing trying to get everything done.

One of her mentors pointed out to her that she was too busy working **in** her business rather than **on** her business. She had no idea what that meant. Her mentor explained to her that she was being reactive to situations rather than being proactive.

What Robyn's mentor explained to her next completely changed the way she ran her business.

There are four types of work that we do:

Urgent and important

For this definition urgent and important are either tasks that can't have been foreseen or ones that have been left by you to do at the last minute. This is very much a reactive state, a constant feel of fire-fighting or crisis management. Types of urgent and important tasks can be emergencies, complaints, demands from customers, unscheduled meetings, staff issues or needs, or problems. When we're working like this constantly we start to feel stressed, anxious, overwhelmed, frantic and worried. Yip, Robyn was definitely in here.

Urgent but not important

These are generally requests from others based on their priorities and expectations, interruptions, and pointless activities.

Not urgent and not important

These are usually distraction activities, e.g. surfing the Internet, social media, playing games, chatting, reading irrelevant material and tidying up your desk. We've all been there!

The most significant contribution you can make to your business is by doing work that is:

Not urgent but important

These activities include:

- Developing systems e.g. instruction manuals, desk files.
- Any type of planning whether that is a simple to do list at the end of the day, or a five-year strategic plan.
- Attending a training course because we're upskilling so that we can do things more effectively and efficiently.
- Undertaking preventative maintenance.
- Research and development.
- Taking a break.
- Taking a holiday.
- Building relationships (Robyn calls this productive socializing!).

Doing these types of activities prevents us from constantly doing urgent and important stuff.

Robyn recognized that she was spending the majority of her time operating in urgent and important. All the not urgent but important tasks she desperately wanted to get to but couldn't because she perceived that she didn't have enough time.

As soon as she took a step back, slowed down and started to do some more strategic planning, undertook training and took time to build relationships, not only did she stop working frantic hours she felt a lot calmer and was able to think more clearly.

She didn't often take a break and wondered why when she got to 3 pm she felt exhausted and very hungry! She didn't take holidays fearing that she would be missing out on valuable income if she took time off. But these activities were important because it gave her the time to refresh, refuel and refocus. Now holidays are scheduled into the calendar at the beginning of the year.

Also Robyn was able to focus on the meaningful parts of the business and get rid of the 'clutter' which freed up her time to take on the clients and work that was really worthwhile.

She stopped running around feeling like a dog trying to catch its tail. It also meant that when she recognized she was starting to do more urgent and important activities that really weren't, she could stop doing them and focus back on the work that really mattered.

As a business owner it's important to say 'yes' and make time for the not urgent but important activities otherwise we'll be forever doing non-urgent and important stuff and reacting.

Summary

Remember the time management big picture: say yes to spending more time doing not urgent but important tasks.

This will help you cope better when you do end up, as we all do, doing the reactive stuff.

Exercise

1. Take a piece of paper and divide it into four squares. Head up each section with: Urgent and Important, Not Urgent but Important, Urgent but not Important, Not Urgent and Not Important.

2. Write down all the things that you're doing into their respective section.

3. Concentrate on the Not Urgent but Important. What is missing? What couple of things could you move to this section that would make sure your working **on** your business not **in** it.

Notes

Part 3 – Stories

We've put these stories in a separate section so you can skip over them if you want. However, just remember, Robyn and Bob are outstanding story tellers so if you skip over our stories, you'll be missing the funny side of running your own business.

Not all of the stories are funny but each story has a point, some of them stated and others obvious.

Running an Event With The Earth Shaking

On 4 September 2010 Christchurch, Canterbury, New Zealand was hit by a 7.1 magnitude earthquake, which caused major damage in the city.

At this time Robyn was six weeks out from running one of her business's key training events for the year, the Southern Secretarial Summit. This was a hugely successful two-day conference that attracted over 100 administrators from all round New Zealand.

Aftershocks continued to rock the city day and night. Some were baby ones and others forced you to take cover under the doorframe or a table, hanging on for dear life while your heart thundered in your chest. However, Cantabrians were doing what they did best. Getting on with it and coping the best they could. Earthquakes would not dent our confidence or prevent us from living our lives.

One day out from the Summit everything was organized and we were on track. My PA and I had some things to pick up from the mall. We were in the supermarket when wham! The ground started shaking, shelves and lightshades swayed and cans hit the floor. The stress of organizing an event under such tiring conditions had finally hit me.

There in the middle of the supermarket I had a meltdown! The ground was shaking and I was shaking. It wasn't the earthquake itself that had bothered me, but that was the straw that broke the camel's back. While my PA comforted me and supermarket staff offered me a cup of tea (tea seems to fix everything!) life was still going on. News travels fast and within moments my cell phone was ringing and beeping as texts and emails were coming in, all with the same message – were we still having the Summit? We had just experienced the biggest aftershock since 4 September (5.0 magnitude, 9 km deep). Power was knocked out in the city and buildings were evacuated.

We had to make a quick decision. The implications of not having the Summit were huge, but we had to consider that this was a serious situation that ultimately could affect people's safety. We took the risk and let everyone know the Summit was still on and we looked forward to seeing them tomorrow!

My PA and I checked into the hotel (on the 19th floor – gulp!) and wondered whether to laugh or cry at the torch (Bob here – a torch is a flashlight to us yanks) beside the bed (to help guide our way out of the hotel in the darkness if the power went off). We were exhausted from our shaky shopping trip and still on high alert. I hoped and prayed that our Summit would go off without a hitch and the earth would be kind to us.

On the morning of the conference registrants arrived excited, but apprehensive.

At the opening the MC did a great job, explaining what the hotel required us to do if an earthquake struck. Take cover and DO NOT evacuate the building until the all clear was given.

At 9.30 am we had an earthquake. Most people felt it, but everyone remained calm. And that, I'm pleased to say, was the only earthquake we had throughout the event.

However, we did have a frightening moment in the afternoon of day two. We were all in the main conference room listening to the presentation. The events team, including myself, was sitting at the back of the room. We were on the mezzanine floor and were about a metre away from the windows which overlooked Cashel Street.

My PA was standing at the back of the room staring out the window and when I looked over to her, I noticed about a million different emotions cross her face, but mainly panic. What was going on? She frantically beckoned to me to look out the window. I did as I saw a lamp post start to slowly tilt in slow motion towards the window.

God, was this a really bad earthquake that was coming but we hadn't yet felt it? I slowly got up out of my seat and joined her at the window. I smiled when I realized what was going on. A road crew was dismantling the lamp post to make way for the tracks being installed for a new tram line. I put my hand to my chest to quiet my thumping heart, as we both watched the lamp post gently being lowered to the ground.

What did I learn from running an event in a seismically active city? Here are some of the things you might want to have if your business includes holding events.

A Risk assessment plan – In today's new reality, this should cover many things including, acts of terrorism and acts of God. These will happen when we least expect them so try to ensure that you and the venue have a plan in place.

A Back-up venue - We were lucky enough that the venue wasn't affected but having a back-up in mind would help if your main one becomes inoperable.

Maintain a Group email - As you register people for your event add them to a group email. This way if you need to contact them, a click of a button will get the message is out quickly.

Health and safety - Make sure everyone has a clear understanding of the emergency procedures.

Cancellation policy - Ensure it's clearly stated on your registration information what the cancellation policy is.

Forward thinking and having robust plans in place will help you to manage whatever may happen during an event. As an event manager it was an experience I hope I don't have to repeat any time soon!

How to Handle Clothing Malfunctions

This story, from Bob's restaurant days, is out of his autobiography.

Several months after we opened, we added a Champagne Sunday Brunch. The first Sunday we offered brunch, our real estate agent, now a good friend, and I were sitting out on the back patio when a little sports car came ripping into the parking lot.

Five minutes later my wife, who was playing hostess that morning, escorted the couple from the sports car out onto the patio. She sat them about four tables from us with the girl facing me and the guy on her left. Thus, I had a perfect full on view of the girl.

The girl had on a pair of *really short* white shorts and a red halter top that barely kept her well-endowed chest covered. He had on... ? (I have no idea what he had on, but it's not important to the story.)

The waitress brought them two glasses of Champagne, and several minutes later came back to take their order. When she finished she came over to our table bent over and whispered to me, "Your wife said to keep an eye on the girl over there".

"Okay. It'll be hard, but I'll try," I said, smiling as the waitress kicked me in the shin. Rubbing my leg, I asked, "Do I get a hint as to why?"

"Church lets out in five minutes and the girl is completely stoned!"

"Ah, okay, I'll keep an eye on her." No sooner did the words leave my mouth when the girl's breasts left her top. As she leaned over to clink glasses with the guy, she had popped out of her top.

Well, I did as I was told and kept an eye on her. Actually, two of them!

The girl looked up at me and smiled, I smiled back and realized she had no idea she was hanging out. It took three tries of lowering my eyes to her breasts and finally nudging the top of my shirt up before she realized what I was trying to tell her.

Looking down, she smiled, pulled her halter top up, winked at me and went on like nothing happened.

Two more pop-outs, now with the church crowd filling most of the patio and I finally had to politely ask them to leave. (Damn! Why me?)

Like Robyn's story, I guess I should have had a risk assessment plan in place and ducked under the table.

A Travel Story

Robyn has travelled too many times to mention in both New Zealand and Australia for business. She has lots of funny stories to tell about her flying adventures.

Here is one of them:

I was waiting at Hamilton Airport for my bags to arrive on the carousel with a woman, called Yvonne, who I was going to be doing some training for.

One of my bags was a backpack which had lots of straps attached.

Just my luck, when it slid down the baggage slide and one of the straps got caught on the conveyer belt. It didn't matter how much Yvonne and I pulled on the strap, it was budged fast. It must have been quite hilarious to see both of us running alongside the conveyer belt trying to free my backpack.

When it disappeared back into the baggage unloading area, we scurried around to the other side of the carrousel to wait so we could have another go at it, much to the enjoyment of all the other passengers.

Another trip around and Yvonne went to get an Air New Zealand representative. When she arrived, she had a go at it, but also couldn't free it. So she said, "Not to worry. I'll get the firefighters."

Um, I'm thinking that's a little dramatic and honestly thought she was joking. But before I had a chance to say anything she was gone.

Five minutes later - three fire fighters turned up with enough equipment to rescue a crashed 747 worth of passengers. I was sooo embarrassed!

Within 30 seconds these lovely firefighters had cut the strap, freeing and rescuing my poor backpack.

They thought it was very funny. Me, kind of, but really, it's hard to laugh when you're busy looking for a door to quietly crawl out of! So I thanked them and sent them off sniggering as Yvonne and I slinked to the nearest exit.

Lessons learned? 1. Never check your backpack. 2. Remember your Girl Scout moto, "Be prepared" and always carry a knife with you. Oops, guess that's not a good idea at the airport. So "Be prepared", to meet a handsome fireman, or two, or three!

Another Travel Story

Bob should start this story by telling you that Robyn and he often swear that they're twins. Even though they live on opposite sides of the world, so many times the same or similar things seem to happen to them. This is one of those times.

I too have travelled a lot for business. On a return trip from British Airways in London, I realized that someone I worked with was on the same flight. He, however, was returning from a golf tournament in Scotland.

While waiting in baggage claim at LAX for my luggage, he came over and asked if I would grab his golf clubs from the carousel while he ran to the restroom. "There's a big lime green ribbon on the handle. Can't miss it. I'm sure I'll be back before they come out. They're always the last things off," he added and off he went.

No sooner had he left when luggage started moving along the upper conveyer belt toward the slide. Several bags slid down and I watched as a golf bag with a big lime green ribbon made its way to the slide behind more suitcases.

As it edged toward the slide, I watched it slowly turning sideways. By the time it reached the top of the slide it was completely sideways and wedged itself between the two sides of the slide. Bag after bag behind it stacked up and hammered the golf bag until it was firmly wedged in.

Finally, an alarm went off, the upper conveyer belt stopped and I watched a guy making his way along it throwing bag after bag to the side. When he got to my friend's golf bag it was impossibly wedged in.

I started to chuckle as he landed the first kick to try and un-wedge it. Second kick, no movement. Third kick, nothing but me and others laughing. Fourth kick, movement and more laughter. Fifth kick and the bag exploded spraying golf clubs, golf balls, tees and who knew what else all over the baggage claim area.

Me? Everyone's laughing and I'm sitting on the side of the carrousel roaring with laughter and hanging on to keep from falling off.

A few minutes later, after his mangled bag and most of his stuff had rotated to the back of the carousel, the guy I worked with walks up. Not really paying much attention, he looks down at me and says, "What's so funny?" Then adds, "Has my golf bag come out yet?"

In between fits of laughter, I reached down, pulled one of his mangled clubs from behind me and handed it to him, adding, "I think you need to go over to the baggage claim window to get the rest."

The good news, unlike Robyn, it wasn't my bag or backpack. The bad news, he somehow failed to see the humor in what happened and actually blamed me.

Lessons learned: 1. Never agree to be responsible for someone else's bag or property unless you have control over them. 2. Good looking firefighters don't always respond to a baggage emergency. Sometimes it a very large gorilla from baggage handling.

Jack and the Doggy Door

This is the story of how Bob's construction business got started.

When he and his first wife got a dog, a small Lhasa Apso, he needed to make sure the dog had a way to get in out of the weather when they were at work.

Simple, install a doggy door in the side door to the garage.

So, one Saturday he was off to Home Depot to purchase a doggy door. Upon returning home, he popped the side garage door off and laid it on his work table so he could cut the hole for the doggy door.

His work table was actually an interior door that he had removed when remodeling their master bedroom and installed a set of folding legs on.

After setting the garage door onto the work table, he laid the doggy door templet on the door, carefully measured everything and marked where he needed to cut. Using the adage of *measure twice, cut once* to make sure the doggy door wouldn't be too high off the floor, he double, then triple checked the distance to the bottom of the doggy door, then proceeded to cut the hole out.

Once he was finished, just to be certain, he lifted the door off the work table and set it in place. As he did, he glanced down at his dog, who had been watching all along, and noticed him staring up at the door with a bewildered look on his face.

Oops! The hole for the doggy door was five feet off the ground!

New motto: *Make sure you've got the right part of the door, then and only then, measure twice and cut once.*

Embarrassed, just as he was setting the door aside so he could go back to Home Depot and buy another door, his neighbor Jack walked by. Jack stopped, looked at the work table then came up the driveway. "Wow, that's a great idea, using a door for a work table," he said.

Quick on his feet, Bob smiled and said, "Yeah. It works really well except for when I cut something. So I just made a new and improved model," while pointing at the ruined side door. "With this one, you can put a paper bag under the hole and when your done cutting something you just use your shop brush to sweep the sawdust through the hole and into the bag.

"That is great! I'll have to make one of those", Jack said.

"Tell you what. Why don't you take this one and I'll just cut a hole in my original work table," Bob told him.

Off Jack went with his new super duper work table while Bob headed for Home Depot and a new side door.

This time though, he lined the door up in the door frame, put a BIG X on the bottom inside and then, and only then, laid the templet on the door.

Just as he was finishing, Jack's wife came over, told Bob how impressed with his ingenuity she was and hired him to help remodel their kitchen. On her way out, she turned, chuckled and asked him, "How long did it take you to think up the story to cover up cutting the hole in the wrong part of the door?"

Deposit Foolery

Bob's restaurant carried three beers on tap and about another five or six in bottles. Once they were up and running Bob told their beer distributer, who only came once a week, to make sure there was always a backup keg of each tap beer in the walk-in out back.

For each keg, there was a $20 deposit on the keg itself, plus the price of the beer. Under normal circumstances, they would have three kegs under the bar, three backup kegs in the walk-in and possibly three empty kegs on the loading dock to be picked up when the beer distributer came next.

That's $60 + $60 + $60 for a total of $180 of their money tied up in keg deposits.

Several months into operating the restaurant, Bob's wife pulled him aside and asked, "What's with all of these keg deposits each month?" Bob looked at the billing and said, "I don't know, let me look into it."

After checking the walk-in and loading dock, he discovered that the driver for the beer distributer had been doubling and tripling up on the backup kegs in the walk-in and not picking up the empty kegs when he made a delivery. In both locations, the kegs had conveniently been placed behind other things so unless you were looking for them, they wouldn't be noticed.

Two hours later the beer distributer was picking up all of his kegs as the new distributer was dropping off his and being warned about never leaving more than six at any given time.

Personalities

In the chapter on personalities, we talk about the four different personality types and Robyn talks a little about how to use them. To give you a better idea, here's the story of how Bob and Robyn use their personalities traits to their advantage as writers.

After working with each other for months on-line and before they met in person, they realized in some ways they were very much alike, (Yeah, scary!) in other ways they were very different. Tying them to the four personality types, Robyn will tell you that Bob has traits from all four. Bob will tell you that the same holds true for Robyn, although she tends to lean more into the Expressive and Amiable areas.

Thus, while they're both romantics and emotional, Bob is very outspoken, and Robyn is more reserved and shy. Being romantics and emotional, ideally suits them in their writing partnership.

However, when it comes to marketing and advertising, Bob takes the lead in public events (book signings, speaking events and writer's conferences) while Robyn provides backup. But, when it comes to on-line events (website development, social media posts, newsletter articles) they switch places, with Robyn taking the lead and Bob backing her up.

The same held true for Bob and his wife when they owned the restaurant, except in this case they are more different then alike. Not opposites, but different enough and fortunately their personalities and ideas always seem to complement each other.

When they had the restaurant, which was his wife's idea, he told her, "This is your idea. I'll support you in every way I can, but you need to take the lead. I'll cook, clean and do any and all repairs, but running the business is your responsibility."

Right! Like that lasted a day… okay, maybe two? Only because the first day he was outside spiffing the place up.

Eventually they did settle into who did what for the day-to-day operations, but business decisions were always decided by both. Why? Not because they didn't trust each other's decisions but because they each looked at things different and thought of different questions. That meant that decisions were made after considering as many options and ramifications as possible.

The Flood Insurance Merry-go-round

Insurance can be confusing and frustrating. As an example, at one point, Bob purchased a house as a rental property. The house was in good condition and close to a college campus; great for keeping the house occupied. Although, as he would quickly learn, bad for Bob's health. Never rent to college students! If you do, burn the house down when they leave.

Back on point. If the college student renters don't get to you, the mortgage lender and insurance companies will. The house he purchased was one block from a flood control channel. Outdated maps showed the property as being in a flood zone. However, a memo from the city declared the area was no longer subject to flooding, thanks to the flood control channel, and stated that the map needed to be updated.

Memo or no memo, the bank refused to approve the loan without a new map or flood insurance. The insurance company, seizing an opportunity, said that without a new map the property was considered to be in a flood zone and quoted a price for flood insurance that made Bob's hair stand on end.

Round and round they went while the house hung in escrow. Finally, Bob threatened to go to the local newspaper and tell them how everyone in the area was illegally being required by the bank to carry flood insurance. Oh, and that the insurance company was complicit.

The city agreed to "expedite" updating their map, which they estimated should be done in about six months to a year. Oh joy! That helps.

Back at the bank and insurance company he leveled the same threat and got both of them to agree to a rider to his policy to cover flooding with a $20,000 deductible. Reluctantly, the bank accepted the rider and seven months later, when the new flood map came out, he cancelled the rider.

Patience and People Skills

Many businesses deal directly with the public and whether you sell a product, a service, or both, patience and good people skills are a must. While you might think this excerpt from Robyn's memoir pretty much covers it all, it probably just touches on the things she often needs to deal with.

Training can be and often is challenging – wrong manuals being printed, wrong venue, wrong room, IT issues, squished into tight rooms, pressure to finish the training on time so I could get to the airport, fire evacuations, cutting out material when falling behind time or adding material when ahead of time, cultural considerations from Maori to a whole class of Arabs, blind and hearing impaired attendees, a woman who was four days overdue from giving birth, drilling outside, drilling inside, injuring myself by falling over in the car park before a session, allowing people to watch major sporting events (e.g. America's Cup, Olympics, Football World Cup), expecting twenty people and only three people turning up, expecting fifteen people and twenty turning up, you name it I've experienced it.

I've also had to deal with people dynamics which included: trying to get a group engaged when it felt like I was teaching the living dead. Worrying that someone was really bored because they were constantly yawning but finding out they'd been nightclubbing until 5 am. Dealing with extroverted attendees who were full on and felt like they were sucking all the energy out of me. And my favorite: the show ponies. These are the people that think the course is all about them and constantly draw attention to themselves by asking question after question and commenting on everything I would say. Personally, I think that these people lack confidence, have low self-esteem and therefore try to overcompensate by going to the extreme.

No matter what or who pops out of the woodwork though, you quickly have to take a deep breath, evaluate it, adjust your game plan and try to maintain your sanity.

Expect the Unexpected

This is another story from Bob's restaurant days. The message? Your best customers can come from the most unexpected places.

On our second brunch Sunday, my wife took a call asking if we had room for a group of thirty for brunch. She assured them we did, as long as they didn't want to sit on the patio. They said they were okay with inside and she called in our backup waitress who lived next door. Then she and one of the waitresses started setting up the front room for them. At the time, only the mayor and his wife were in the room and they were almost finished.

Fifteen minutes later the most God-awful roar filled the parking lot as twenty to twenty-five Harleys and trikes pulled in. It turned out the call was from a biker club from the next town who were also friends of the previous owner.

Just as they pulled in, two little old ladies came running through the door and one yelled out, "Call the Sherriff! There's hundreds of Hells Angels in the parking lot!"

My wife calmed the women down, assured them the biker's reservation was only for thirty, and they were not Hell's Angels. Then she escorted the women to the patio. She returned to the hostess station just as the bikers came in and the mayor and his wife went out.

The bikers turned out to be one of the best groups we ever had. They were amazed that they had their own room, already set up and two waitresses assigned just to them. The men ordered Coronas, the women mimosas and together they ate enough food to feed a large third world country for a year. Within an hour I was off on the first of three trips to the local market to replenish Corona, orange juice, jalapenos, cheddar cheese and sourdough bread.

They ended up spending over four hours in the restaurant. Not only were they exceptionally polite, the two waitresses ended up with at least twice as much in tips as they would have made in the main dining room or patio.

They also became *regulars* for Sunday Brunch.

Go Ahead, Make My Day

Not all reviews are bad and it's that one good review that often makes it all worthwhile.

Out of all the training stories, it's the ones where somebody went out of their way to take the time to give Robyn some feedback.

This is a sample of one of the letters received from a participant who attended her personal assistant courses.

"Over a year ago I attend two of Robyn's courses – The Outstanding Personal Assistant and Professional Minute Taking, both having a profound impact on where I am today.

When I went on these two courses I was on secondment positions as a PA and lacked confidence in my abilities as I had this perception that the position PA/EA was like the holy grail of administration roles. I had come from a strong administrative background and was new to this field then the questioning of transferable skills.

After attending your courses I came away feeling wow – I am doing this and yes it is so achievable and how limiting my self-doubts were. I applied for a role at X which is setting up the new super city council and I now look after eight managers and their supporting project and programme managers.

As time progresses closer to the changeover date, I decided I wanted to have some control over my future direction. I applied for a PA role at an equally high and professional level and have successfully been offered the position.

I wanted to say thank you for the incredible impact your course had on me and which also encouraged me to be explorative seeking out reference material to assist and empower my abilities. I am sending two lovely books I ordered on-line which I wanted to 'pay forward' either as reference guides for yourself or as a gift to a student that you feel would benefit.

Thank you once again and keep up the wonderful work you are doing as the ripples do go far and wide.

No matter how much of a bad day I might've had, it was feedback like this that made it all worthwhile.

Yay! The End

Conclusion

As Porky Pig would say, "That's all folks!"

(or was that Daffy Duck?)

Well everyone, thanks for sticking with us to the end.

We hope that you've found the information helpful, our stories inspiring and we've motivated you to get going on your dream.

We've enjoyed sharing our experiences and having you join us along the way.

We wish you all the best in your endeavors of running your own business. It's not easy, in fact it's downright hard work, but the rewards – monetary and intrinsic – are well worth the journey and… you'll be less likely to fail in business without even trying!

Would you like to send us some feedback? We'd love to hear from you – how helpful you found our book and how it assisted you in business. Our contact details are on the acknowledgement page.

Heaps of best wishes.

Robyn and Bob

Acknowledgments

Our thanks to television shows like: Restaurant Impossible, Restaurant Stakeout, Bar Rescue, Hotel Rescue and other business "rescue" shows for inspiring this book.

To Robyn, from Bob: Thanks for threatening me with bodily harm if I didn't finish what I'd started so many years ago. And for adding so much that I hadn't even thought of. Having you as my co-author got me excited again (not like that!) about the value we could provide to small business owners

To Bob, from Robyn: Glad I could help get your butt into gear and help you finally finish. Oh, and get you excited again! It's been a hoot!

Special thanks to Bob's wife Sheryl, and Alicia Melbourne in England, for wading through several drafts, offering wonderful suggestions and pointing out things we'd missed. Were it not for them, our book would only be ten pages long. Well, maybe eleven pages.

Finally, thanks to Anita Lewis, Tricia Caughley, Alicia Melbourne and Carly Fangey for their advanced reviews.

For feedback, please contact Robyn or Bob via bobboze70@gmail.com or booksinthevines@gmail.com

For other books written and published by Bob and Robyn, and links to their social media sites, check out their websites:

Bob: https://bobboze.com for their Romance stuff and

Robyn: www.minutesmadness.wordpress.com for her business stuff

www.ingramcontent.com/pod-product-compliance
Lightning Source LLC
Chambersburg PA
CBHW051306220526
45468CB00004B/1226